AMERICAN TRADEMARK DESIGNS

A SURVEY WITH 732 MARKS, LOGOS AND CORPORATE-IDENTITY SYMBOLS

by Barbara Baer Capitman

DOVER PUBLICATIONS, INC., NEW YORK

Published in Canada by General Publishing Company, Ltd., 30 Lesmill Road, Don Mills, Toronto,
Ontario.
Published in the United Kingdom by Constable
and Company, Ltd., 10 Orange Street, London WC 2.

American Trademark Designs is a new work,
first published by Dover Publications, Inc., in 1976.

International Standard Book Number: 0-486-23259-X
Library of Congress Catalog Card Number: 75-44714

Manufactured in the United States of America
Dover Publications, Inc.
180 Varick Street
New York, N.Y. 10014

PREFACE

This pictorial review comes out at a time of problems and uncertainty for the commercial design profession. Although there has never been such a wealth of wit and technical virtuosity as that shown by today's graphic artists, many familiar trademarks are in trouble. This is not because there is anything inherently wrong with the marks themselves, but rather because the public has come to think of them as synonymous with the *identity* of the particular institutions they represent. Economic, political, social factors—remote from the graphic merits of the designs—are deciding whether trademarks are equal to the Herculean job assigned them: to endow their owners with positive imagery. Watergate, multinational trade, ethnic struggles, ecological debates and consumerism are among the issues that have become part of the current trademark's connotations.

The majority of designers and graphic artists still reject this concept of the trademark as indivisible from the relationship of its possessor to the public. They prefer to think of themselves as technicians whose sole concern is with strong, clear and esthetically satisfying visual impressions. Despite the advances of social psychology and visual perception, most of the design world is not involved with the complexities of trademark meaning.

The brighter side of this picture is that although some big corporation marks may now have dis-
turbing and/or negative connotations, the skill used to evolve and promote trademarks into familiar symbols is currently being used for broader purposes. There have never been so many exciting and well-executed symbols for small businesses and professions, local enterprises and nonprofit institutions. There is increasing use of trademarks for political organizations, international conferences, schools, hospitals, museums, festivals, directional signage, fund drives and similar purposes.

As this collection shows, the talent focused on a regional resort or charitable activity is frequently of the same high caliber as that used for the most intensively researched and supported corporate-identity program. There appears to be mounting enthusiasm for and appreciation of good typography, creative graphics and distinctive symbolism, as well as widespread recognition of the fact that a strong trademark can be helpful to almost any venture.

Color, animation, illumination and adaptability to many applications, media and sizes are important factors in establishing the memorability of a trademark. Some of the examples reproduced here in black and white seem almost novel stripped of their more familiar dimensions or colors. But a rule of thumb seems to be that if a trademark works well in black and white, it is also apt to work in other guises.

I wish to thank the hundreds of designers and

corporate-design directors who helped to put this material together. But this volume is dedicated to my husband, William G. Capitman, who was most involved in it before his untimely death in July, 1975. As president of the Center for Research in Marketing, he constantly urged designers to realize that theirs was far from a narrow craft, but rather one most intimately bound up with the dynamics of our society.

BARBARA BAER CAPITMAN

Miami, February, 1976

INTRODUCTION

Just before the turn of the century, as financial panic gripped the country, William H. Danforth, just out of St. Louis University, was advised by his father to "get into a business that fills a need for lots of people—something they'll need all year around in good and bad times." Since horse and mule stores dotted every corner, as gas stations do today, Danforth joined two other young businessmen to manufacture feed in 1894.

Four years later, convinced that the cereal germ that was always removed in order to prevent rancidity was actually beneficial to human health, Danforth found a miller who could make cracked wheat, and sold it as Purina Whole Wheat Cereal, a name derived from the company slogan, "where purity is paramount." In 1902, teaming up with Dr. Ralston, a popular health-food advocate of the period, Danforth renamed the business the Ralston Purina Company.

This was the same year that, casting about for an "appropriate dress" for his products, he remembered that as a boy, when he worked in his father's Charleston, Missouri, store, every Saturday he had watched the Brown family come to town, all dressed in red and white checks cut from the same bolt of cloth. Since then the checkerboard design (now spelled with a capital C in company releases) has been used for many decades with a consistency unique in American business. Even the company address in St. Louis is known as Checkerboard Square.

As the company grew, Danforth became increasingly evangelistic about his own Horatio Alger-like life, and demanding in his expectations for his employees and products. The checkerboard became a mystical symbol for a "four-square plan": "stand tall, think tall, smile tall, live tall."

Perhaps the most important part of this story for the student of trademarks is the fact that in the minds of Purina's many publics—the farmers who went to the feed store for its chow, the kids who grew up on its cereals, the investors who bought its stocks, the employees, wholesalers, readers of magazines—the checkerboard design became an integral part of the Purina image. Today few people know who Danforth was or much about the wide range of products this over-56-million-dollar firm produces. But most Americans, and many people around the world, upon seeing the checkerboard symbol have immediate associations of old-fashioned, rural, pet-centered plentifulness.

This is both the power and the purpose of trademarks: to bring into our minds a set of positive associations for a complex, vast, essentially impersonal enterprise. These visual symbols are the closest a giant corporation can come to anthropomorphizing itself, to presenting a face, a personality; they are a way of bringing into being something that is enormously far-reaching, complicated, many-faceted, and in many cases not even tangible.

As more people come to realize the ability of trademarks to perform this function, or series of functions, ranging from recognition and recall to improving the image of a product or service, trademarks increasingly compete for a place in the minds of the publics they address.

For the contemporary designer, the task of producing a trademark that is uniquely associated with his client and that evokes an immediate set of positive connotations becomes more difficult as trademark use becomes more widespread. The new symbol designed by Lippincott & Margulies to mark the National Broadcasting Company's 50th anniversary of network broadcasting is, perhaps, the most dramatic example of the growing difficulties in finding a unique solution. This trademark, two simple geometric forms—one red, one blue—that combine to form the letter N, was the result of a corporate-identity program that reputedly cost millions of dollars. The company was recently embarrassed to discover that a small Nebraska public broadcasting company had come up with the same mark—at a cost of less than $200!

More such duplications may be expected. Even in these pages there are examples of different industries and companies with very similar designs. Repetition seems inevitable when trademarks are so much a part of the consciousness of both industrial and nonindustrial societies, of both the aged and pre-schoolers who still can't read but play with their Green Giant dolls, of both *Wall Street Journal* readers and subscribers to the underground press. Trademarks are the applied design on planes that wing to the least developed parts of the globe; they lend confidence to technicians who open packages in the most sophisticated hospital operating theatres. They glow on highways, appear as supergraphics on buildings, serve as designs for fashionable luggage and clothing. The applications are countless. In many instances marks have meaning beyond the products they stand for—as a Playboy symbol pasted on a Corvette becomes a symbol for a life style. Such offshoot applications go far beyond Mr. Danforth's personal statement about his product.

Nevertheless, trademarks still have a sales function as a major job. When a designer creates a trademark his main task is not to produce an attractive piece of art, an abstract or symbolic design that can be worn as a personal ornament or used as an applied decoration; rather it is to find a shorthand way of communicating about the product or service. Still, he must bear in mind that the trademark will be used in countless forms.

A designer of a new mark for a school, for example, will have in mind that it will be worn by athletes on uniforms, by students on patches and T-shirts, and be printed on stationery, notebooks, blankets, ashtrays and jewelery. It will be used on car stickers and for advertising and recruitment purposes. From its many applications come sets of both psychological and technical criteria. The design must reflect the dignity and tradition of the institution as well as its forward-looking aspects; it must be sophisticated enough to convey the idea of a quality education and yet not be stuffy. Technically it must be simple enough to be reproducible in many forms and yet keep its design integrity and clarity. It must be legible and memorable.

To search pattern books for armorial bearings, mythological figures or new letter forms was, at one time, a good way to begin. Today's designer is more likely to start with the formulation of a "design platform"—a researched statement as to which segments of the population the trademark is meant to serve and what personality characteristics it should convey.

Most of the marks in this book were developed in this way. Some are successful because they have long histories and have become meaningful as part of American tradition. Others are breaking new ground for their recent owners, and have been designed to impress themselves upon a public consciousness already saturated with visual impressions.

In the second half of the seventies we are witnessing simultaneous divergent trends in trademark design that have to do with the problems of the economy and the new goals of the society. These trends also reflect both an advanced technical proficiency and a revival of interest in older lettering styles and graphic techniques.

The following brief historical analysis of trademark design will perhaps help to explain how these trends are working.

The Older Trademark as Franchise

The older trade symbols, such as Purina's Checkerboard, are still used and cherished by their possessors as valuable business commodities. Marketers and designers today bend their efforts to retaining trademarks in which companies have a vested interest, while modifying them to make them more contemporary and adaptable to applications such as TV advertising or signage. This effort can backfire when the genuine historicity or authenticity is lost, and a prized piece of Americana then becomes just another mark. Metropolitan Life Insurance finally gave up its tower symbol, and Mobil Oil, after struggling long and hard with the problem of how to handle its winged horse, Pegasus, has practically discontinued its use.

One tends to forget how much a part of the visual surroundings trademarks were even in the days before mass distribution. They were seen on posters and packaging, on freight cars and company banners, were painted three stories high on city buildings and country barns, and became in many instances very much a part of the folklore and mythology of everyday life.

"Trade figures" (marks based on animals or human figures) in particular were impressed on the American consciousness. In the Buster Brown Museum in New York City, for example, Buster Brown and his dog Tige are represented as puppets and dolls and on umbrellas, needle cases, cutouts, candy molds, tops and other "antique" memorabilia. Children still go to sleep clutching trade-figure dolls, and a study done at Columbia University in 1957 showed that trade-figure marks become part of children's consciousness before the alphabet does.

In 1966 the Center for Research in Marketing conducted a study on the character of Mr. Boh, a figure then used widely by the National Bohemian Brewing Company in Baltimore. Research showed that beer drinkers could fantasize at great length over what was essentially a rather sparely drawn image, merely because Mr. Boh was always illustrated with one eye and therefore seemed to have a lovable human weakness.

Studies of other trade characters and figures —from Trade and Mark (the Smith Brothers cough-drop founders) to Chessie (the drowsy Chesapeake railroad cat asleep on a pillow) and Elsie, the Borden cow (and her family); from Psyche (the White Rock beverage muse) to the Campbell Kids and the Dutch Cleanser girl, perhaps the most compulsive house cleaner of all time—all revealed a longing on the part of manufacturers to escape the depersonalization and sameness of consumer products, and an equal readiness on the part of consumers to use trademarks to differentiate between brands and companies.

There were other notable early marks which are included in these pages:
  —the Whitman Sampler "messenger boy"
  —the Santa Fe Railroad shield, initiated by a customer's agent
  —La Belle Chocolatière, found by Walter Baker in Switzerland
  —the Sherwin-Williams globe with its dripping paintbrush
  —the Brooks Brothers lamb
  —the W. & J. Sloane thistle
  —the Sunshine baker

Imbued with the spirit of personal salesmanship, the founding families of corporations drew on their travels, their background in the arts and mythology, and native humor to promote their products with visual symbolism. This primitive approach has lasted for some time. The Reynolds Aluminum trademark based on Raphael's "St. George and the Dragon," produced in 1935 at the suggestion of company founder R. S. Reynolds, Sr., after a trip abroad, is still in use. Sterling Morton created the Morton Salt girl, and the son of the president of Dwight & Church, a Yale graduate who invented baking soda, brought his spice firm to his father with its trademark—Vulcan's arm with hammer.

Another example of this personal interest taken by early entrepreneurs in the design of product and trademark is told in William Cahn's commissioned book, Out of the Cracker Barrel, the Nabisco Story. The National Biscuit Company's Adolphus Green not only found the flaky soda cracker he was convinced people would enjoy and clipped its corners to enhance handling and preservation, but also interested himself actively in nomenclature and promotion. According to Cahn, after the Chicago World's Fair of 1893 millions of people were interested in new designs, inventions and manufacturers and there was a new rush to identify products. This new public was "friends" of the curly-headed boy of Hires Root Beer and of the Scott's Emulsion cod-liver-oil fisherman with the huge fish over his shoulder. Green, working with N. W. Ayer, his advertising agency in Philadelphia, developed the trade figure of the round-cheeked boy in the rain slicker. But, near the turn of the century, Green became obsessed with a desire for a new, abstract visual symbol for his company. He spent night after night thumbing through the books in his personal library until he came across a volume on Italian Renaissance printers' symbols. One was a cross with two bars and an oval, used in the fifteenth century by the Society of Printers in Venice. He selected this as the Nabisco trademark and asked Frederic W. Goudy, then a young Philadelphia artist, to design the logotype for the National Biscuit Company. It was adopted by the company in 1900, and the most recent of six minor changes was done in 1958 by Raymond Loewy.

Style and Modern Art

The thirties and very early forties, before World War II, saw the development of modern advertising with a more self-conscious use of product identification involving the employment of artists to work on corporate design and institutional identities. The Birds Eye bird; the Canada Dry globe; Elsie, the Borden Cow; the Dutch Boy Paint figure were some of the results of this period. Also, from 1915 on, monograms and calligraphic motifs were used more self-consciously as artistic devices. Rohm and Haas, the chemical company, in 1916 had such a "modern" monogram floating above a series of twelve wavy lines. The company says its precise design attribution has been lost with time but that the design was by a "German professor," no doubt a precursor of the intellectual migration from Europe that was later to have such impact on American industrial design.

The work of Ben Shahn, for example, who returned to the depression-torn U. S. A. from study in Europe, has had tremendous effect on graphic designers. In his book *About Letters and Lettering* (New York, 1963) he speaks of the interrelationship of letters and spaces, and of how, by studying lithographic engraving, he learned that "each line of letters had to be a unit, to form a single and not a scattered silhouette, to be balanced by the eye."

Bauhaus influence was to show up in the trademarks of the thirties and forties—boxes and circles with geometric forms influenced by Peggy Guggenheim's collection of geometric art. In industrial applications, particularly, there was an attempt to make trademarks capture the gestalt of the new streamlined products being sold and of the new materials and technology being marketed.

Post-World War II Design; the Era of Industrial Design

In the immediate postwar period the industrial designers set out full-force to sell American business on design as a sales tool. Graphics were considered just one aspect of the designer's mission, and "cleaning up" existing trademarks and developing new ones for use in conjunction with new products and services appearing on the market became integral aspects of the graphic designer's job, just as streamlining a locomotive or putting a new housing on a jigsaw was part of the industrial designer's work.

In the forties and fifties, Raymond Loewy's office turned out the International Harvester mark; Paul Rand designed the IBM mark; Herbert Matter changed the look of the New York, New Haven & Hartford Railroad with a new logotype; and Royal Dadmun designed the Diamond Alkali mark. Morton Goldsholl, still imbued with the teachings of Hans Hofmann, went on to design the Motorola M and the three interlocking diamonds of the IMC mark.

The trademark was often seen primarily as a function of packaging; as the supermarket developed, packaging became more important each year, and the trademark function was to persuade the consumer that a reputable company stood behind the product. In the thirties, packages had been used as trademarks, particularly in advertising, and William Golden (CBS art director until his death in 1961) spoke about the artists' battle to liberate layout from stereotyped ads featuring packages, used as trademarks, in the bottom corner. On television products were sold by showing the complete package, seldom the trademark itself.

The Development of Corporate Identity

The fifties and the sixties saw several developments. One was the growth of multinational corporations and the accompanying spread of corporate mergers. The change in the pattern of business, with ownership of corporations by finance capital, resulted in a de-emphasis on specific, narrowly defined trademarks to stand for a few products or branches of an organization. At this time many well-known trade figures were dropped; magazine articles lamented the putting to pasture of Borden's Elsie and Mobil's Pegasus.

A second new development centered around a newly felt need to modernize and "clean up" old marks in order to get them to better express the great size and forcefulness of the new business concerns. Ubiquity became the name of the game as new marks appeared on the tails of planes, on manhole covers, calling cards, hang tags, tie clips, match covers and T-shirts.

Other new developments were the appearance and success of design firms specializing in "corporate-identity systems" and, in the sixties, increasing use of "books of standards," as it became a first principle that trademarks must be used *consistently* in all applications.

By 1970, when American Telephone and Telegraph began to apply Saul Bass's new telephone symbol in what was then the largest corporate-identity job ever done, it was thought necessary to bring out a *set* of standards books, one each for architecture, fleet, stationery, advertising, and so on.

In 1963, Tom Geismar of Chermayeff & Geismar designed the Chase Manhattan symbol, a square inscribed in an octagon. This became a model for many trademarks which followed because, apparently simple though really sophisticated (its art sources lay in the geometrics of Léger and Mondriaan), it was capable of many variations.

Following up on the important contributions of Ben Shahn and other calligraphers—and of Herb Lubalin, in particular—designers came to place new stress on the name itself as a symbol, and to make corporate names both more memorable and more decorative, they were often shortened. Thus Lippincott & Margulies in 1964 abbreviated the name of New York Life Insurance Company to New York Life and set closely spaced white letters in a black square. This eventually became known as the "stacked" lettering style, and as this volume shows it is now felt to be equally right for bank logos and intimate cafés.

By the end of the sixties it had become clear that certain industries were more prone to trademark use and promotion than others. Insurance companies, banks, financial houses of all kinds and land developers were among the categories of companies that used this form of visual promotion in a large way because they were selling intangibles. The oil industry also became highly conscious of the importance of trademarks to marketing efforts. In the mid-fifties, designers systematically swept through this industrial area, researching consumers' awareness of and association with various trademarks, and suggesting redesign to the companies. This activity was capped in 1973 with Loewy/Snaith's design of the Exxon sign, used by 25,000 former Esso stations and advertised as a name change in "saturation advertising" from coast to coast.

Monograms and abstract symbols became pre-dominant and the design of the mark frequently did not identify the nature of the company or product. There was, and is, often no difference between a hotel symbol and a clothing symbol, a bank symbol and a symbol for an automobile parts supply house. Designers and companies, too, are caught in a self-inflicted dilemma: whether to create designs that approximate contemporary fine art, the kind of designs that Paul Rand eloquently urged in all his books, or to "pander" to the popular preference for representationalism, Victorian gimcrackery and whacky humor that essentially says, along with the advertisers themselves at the 1971 FTC hearings on advertising, "we were only spoofing—we never thought anyone would believe us."

The Period of Low Corporate Profile

The economic and social ills of the post-Watergate era had their effect on corporate symbolism and on other types of trademarks as well. The period 1969–71 was the period of "low corporate profile." Corporations spoke of the necessity for social involvement and hesitated to let it be known that sometimes millions of dollars were spent just to introduce a new trademark. Design studios cut their staffs to the bone, and it was the "underground," imperfect, casual look that succeeded in trademarks as well as in other areas of advertising. Such cozy motifs as John Held, Jr.'s twenties flapper figures and Tiffany glass Art Deco sunbursts were used to embellish trademarks. In an effort to look personal and carefully crafted, rather than coldly and perfectly mass-produced, logotypes harked back to antique hand-lettered styles, in imitation of the Gothics so admired by William Morris and the Pre-Raphaelite Brotherhood.

But in 1972 the heavy, substantial, abstracted look of corporate symbolism began to return, and there came with it increased design activity. In January, 1976, the trademark register announced a record of 2,000 new or renewed trademarks in one month. Names continued to be shortened, as part of the corporate style. Sperry Rand became Sperry; Mobil Gas became Mobil; computer-like names were found, such as TICOR, a giant financial and leasing firm that ended up in financial trouble, along with some of the other land speculators whose marks are to be found here. The American Stock Exchange adopted a heavy circular brandmark suggestive of the trading pit, and became AMEX.

On the other hand, as we have noted, the

corporations began to return to the past in search of the old-fashioned values sought by the public. Quaker Oats clung to its time-honored Quaker figure in an abstracted head designed by Saul Bass even though the company is now the Quaker Company, a broad concern with many divisions. Similarly, the American Tobacco Company, in a conscious effort to diversify after the Surgeon General's report, became American Brands, Inc., and modernized its product line and services but retained its Indian-head trademark. And Buster Brown, the comic-strip character from the twenties, is still being actively exploited by the Buster Brown Shoe Company aside from that Museum of Memorabilia in New York. The Green Giant, the Morton Salt girl, the Land O Lakes Indian girl, the Planters Peanut man—all these trade figures are once again being heavily backed by their companies with an endless parade of gimmicks and promotions built around them, ranging from a motel chain's sleepy bear rag doll to an increasing use of animation and realism that is even taking the trademark out of the hands of designers altogether. Thus we now find the Hartford deer or the Dreyfus lion stalking eerily across television screens, while an Allstate Insurance representative cups his hands and intones, "You're in good hands with Allstate."

The Power of Trademarks

Collected trademarks can be reviewed in three different ways: (1) as interesting historic memorabilia; (2) as examples of graphic designs; and (3) as tokens of extraordinarily successful or heavily promoted marketing efforts. This collection takes all these aspects into account. But the total effect created by such a large collection of trademarks is the recognition of the potency of this visual shorthand. In a period in which we have all become much more aware of large corporations and institutions, it is amazing how much a small black-and-white modern-day iconograph can convey in terms of history, goals, standards and public affairs. Market research on Monsanto's trademark in the early sixties revealed that looking at this simple M letter form evoked a chain of reactions, not immediately produced but lying quite close to the surface, concerning war and munitions makers, big business, and so forth. These feelings can be highly subjective: a Ford owner who buys a "lemon" will have a negative reaction to the Ford oval and logotype; an IBM stockholder who makes money and holds on to

it will view the IBM typewriter-face mark with affection.

As large institutions, such as banks, for example, lose some of their hitherto unquestionable position of strength and power in the eyes of the public, one wonders what their symbols, which were carefully designed to encompass personality characteristics of authority and leadership, will eventually come to mean. In a recent *New York Times* story headlined "Bank Concerns on 'Problem' List at Federal Reserve a Year Ago," five bank marks and logotypes were reproduced with no discrimination made between the banks and their marks. In fact, the caption read, "Some of the bank holding companies in the more serious category of the Federal Reserve's 'problem' list," as though it were providing positive and full identification of the firms involved.

Still, if a trademark *is* the institution and has this power to become the *face* of the institution, then a trademark also has the power to affect public feeling toward its possessor.

Consider the case of the Cities Service Oil Company. In the late fifties research showed the old design, a trefoil, to have poor connotations in attributes important to gas stations (efficient service, cleanliness, honest pricing, and so on). A well-considered design change produced the now familiar triangle. This design was so intimately connected with the growth of the company that the whole image of the brand changed. It not only became the sign of a major oil company but on each criterion of effectiveness its position improved radically.

Iconography and Design

The iconography with which a trademark accomplishes all these amazing feats of association is hard to separate from the trademark itself. It is a study of the history of symbolism and symbols. Yet trademarks have traditionally relied on symbolism. Early trademarks drew heavily on the imagery of the sea and agriculture—anchors, clipper ships, tridents, mermaids, wheat stalks, leaves, barns, farmyard animals—and on heraldic devices. The associations were thought to be automatic: farm symbols meant purity; heraldic symbols implied status. This was true for butter or beer, a car or a can of paint. This basic vocabulary of symbolism still forms much of the stock-in-trade of the designer.

But the design movement away from representationalism has led to the use of lettering styles and lines that have an iconography of their own. The old symbolism of classical mythology, religion, nationalism and so forth has been partially replaced by the new symbolism of corporate values—ubiquity, modernity, efficiency, leadership.

Today more than ever before designers are involved with calligraphy and typography to achieve the desired effect through manipulation of lines and solid forms and space. Perhaps, however, the most important stylistic element of contemporary trademark design is the use of space. This derives in part from the constructivist paintings, such as those of El Lissitzky, the Russian whose posters experimented with geometric negative and positive boundaries.

Ultimately, one design after another shown here derives, as in modern art, from the interplay of void and solid. This aspect can become the major fascination if the designs are looked at in terms of gamesmanship or wit, and it is the clever use of space that, more than anything else, sets the contemporary symbol apart from its more linear or sculptural predecessors.

The preoccupation with space as form is evident in any examination of contemporary abstract painting—for example in the work of Arshile Gorki. In Gorki's final abstract painting style (1944–48) space becomes pure extension. The image is balanced against emptiness which it invades or disappears into. Modern painting also supplied the concept of the "double image." In surrealist painting, such as Dali's work, this meant that the representation of an object became, without the slightest physical change, also the representation of another entirely different object. When abstractionists such as Gorki condensed two or more images, the surviving aspects of the component image or images retained sufficient power to evoke the complete original images. This multiple-meaning imagery in painting, at first infuriating to the public, in time became acceptable, and paved the way to understanding the possibility that a trademark can also have layers of meaning. Today, when trademarks which at first glance appear to be very simple are often in fact extremely sophisticated and elegant in their iconography and design, a large public has developed the ability to appreciate them quite fully and to recognize their often very complex public and private meanings.

BIBLIOGRAPHY

Burns, Aaron, *Typography*. New York, 1961.

Cahn, William, *Out of the Cracker Barrel, the Nabisco Story*. New York, 1969.

Capitman, William G., *A Study of Consumer Response to Oil Company Gas Station Signs*. Peekskill, New York, 1957.

Capitman, William G., "In the Valley of Decision," *Industrial Design*. April, 1974.

Dadmun, Royal, *Insurance Company Symbolism, A Market Research Study*. Baltimore, 1964.

Ferebee, Ann, *A History of Design from the Victorian Era to the Present*. New York, 1970.

Golden, Cipe Pineles, *The Visual Craft of William Golden,* edited also by Kurt Weihs and Robert Strunsky, New York, 1962.

Hambidge, Jay, *Dynamic Symmetry*. Providence (Rhode Island School of Design), 1961. (Dover reprint.)

Hofmann, Armin, *Graphic Design Manual,* with introduction by George Nelson. New York, 1965.

Koch, Rudolf, *The Book of Signs*. New York, 1965. (Dover reprint.)

Lehner, Ernst, *Symbols, Signs and Signets*. Cleveland, 1950. (Dover reprint.)

Lippincott, J. Gordon, *Design for Business*. Chicago, 1947.

Lippincott, J. Gordon, *Designing a Brandmark for Today's Market*. New York (Lippincott & Margulies, Inc.), 1956.

Loewy, Raymond, *Never Leave Well Enough Alone*. New York, 1951.

Rand, Paul, *Thoughts on Design*. New York, 1947.

Shahn, Ben, *About Letters and Lettering (Love and Joy about Letters)*. New York, 1963.

Whittock, Arnold, *Symbols for Designers*. London, 1935.

also:

Corporate Identity (a newsletter), 1969–71.

Graphics, New York, 1968–73.

Industrial Design, 1968, 1969, 1973.

Twenty-Seven Chicago Designers (an annual), Chicago, 1965.

U & lc (a newspaper), 1975–76.

CONTENTS

ENTERTAINMENT, LEISURE, SPORTS
(Including Hotels and Restaurants)

The world of entertainment is so varied—in form, in location, in mood—that one can only show a few representative examples. These range from the "underground" humor of Tiffany's Attic (Fig. 81), a Kansas City nightspot, to the classic abstraction of the CBS "eye" (Fig. 18). Sports trademarks, of course, have a life of their own, appearing on the sails of boats, the gut in tennis rackets, the housings of motors, and the shirts of owners! Many of these marks are typically active-looking. Some hotel marks were chosen because of their unrelenting ubiquity; others—Santa Fe's Bishop's Lodge (Fig. 60), for example—for their dignity. And restaurant marks range from the familiar, straightforward Howard Johnson's peaked roof (Fig. 82) to the elegantly abstracted Four Seasons' trees (Fig. 35). This group of marks is quite thematic in approach since the "product" is narrowly defined. We have included many of Saul Bass's early film title marks, which opened up whole new areas, television and film, to graphic designers.

1

2

3

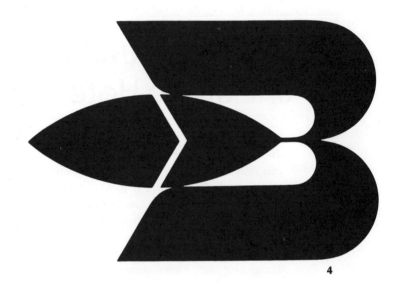

4

5

6

1. Regatta Club. Designed in 1973 by The Brothers Bogusky. 2. Tanglewood Concert Series. Designed in 1969 by Jerome Schuerger. 3. The Kings Contrivance, an inn. 4. Buffalo Braves, N.B.A. Designed in 1971 by Mel Richman, Inc. 5. WQED / WQEX, Channel 2, Public Service TV, Pittsburgh, Pa. Designed by Ken Cooke, now with CBS. 6. National Hockey League Players Association. Designed in 1972 by Lee Payne. 7. Tonio's, a restaurant, a division of Lawry's. Designed by Saul Bass & Associates, Inc. 8. WRKO, a Boston radio station that appeals to a youthful audience. 9. Quebec Aces, A.H.L. Designed in 1970 by Mel Richman, Inc. 10. Driver New Boats, Inc. Designed in 1957 by The Brothers Bogusky. 11. Waldo Astoria. Designed in 1973 by John Quastler Associates, Inc. 12. Sports Films & Talents. Representational approach, a bronze Victory against a length of film. Designed in 1972 by William O. Twet.

7

8

9

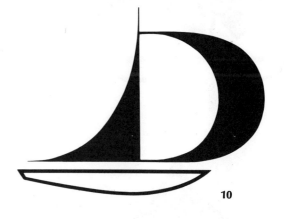

10

11

12

13

THE FIREMENS BALL

14

15

16

WARNER COMMUNICATIONS

17

18

19

20

21

the Misfits

22

13. Philadelphia 76'ers, N.B.A. Designed in 1968 by Mel Richman, Inc. **14.** "The Firemen's Ball." Trademark for the film in every sense of the word. Designed by Saul Bass & Associates, Inc. **15.** AYH Bicycle Mark. Bicycle symbol developed by American Youth Hostels, 1970. **16.** Sahara Hotel. Designed in 1960 by Gould & Associates, Inc. **17.** Warner Communications. New symbol designed by Saul Bass & Associates, Inc. **18.** CBS, Columbia Broadcasting System. William Golden's eye symbol for CBS was designed in 1958 primarily for use on the air to distinguish CBS-TV from radio, but it has since been used in an endless variety of forms and for many purposes. It is a credit to his genius that it has never become tiresome or dated. **19.** "Grand Prix." Title for the John Frankenheimer film by Saul Bass, which captures the motion of the racing cars. The designer shot much of the footage in this film. **20.** Girves Brown Derby, restaurant chain. First version, 1962. Redesigned in 1972 by Al Margolis of Lang, Fisher & Stashower. **21.** AMF, manufacturers of sporting equipment. Name was changed from American Machine Foundry. First version, 1970. New trademark with triangle over M designed in 1971 by Anspach, Grossman, Portugal, Inc. **22.** "The Misfits." Trademark for the United Artists film, designed by George Nelson & Co., Inc. **23.** RCA, Radio Corporation of America, "His Master's Voice." "Nipper," painting by Francis Barrand, used as RCA trademark since 1900.

23

PARKER OUTDOOR WORLD

25

TICKETRON

24

27

26

28

24. Ticketron, Inc., the "electronic box office." Capital T formed by computer printout symbols. Designed by Edward Lampert Associates. **25.** Parker Outdoor World, a sports and recreation center. Designed in 1973 by deMartin-Marona & Associates, Inc. **26.** Reeves Broadcasting Corporation. Designed in 1968 by Ken Saco / Curt Loewy, Inc. **27.** General Cinema Corporation. The GCC forms a projector. Designed in 1966 by Selame Design Associates. **28.** Warner Bros. 50th Anniversary. Has the Art Deco flavor of the early films. Designed by Saul Bass & Associates, Inc. **29.** New Jersey Sports Complex. Designed in 1973 by Peter Muller-Munk Associates, Inc. **30.** Walt Disney World. Official trademark designed by the Disney organization. **31.** Hilton Hotels Corporation. Designed in 1967 by Bill Bossert. **32.** Red Carpet Inns of America, Inc. 1969. **33.** Best Western Motels, an organization of 1200 motels. Designed in 1961 by the founder, M. K. Guertin.

30

29

31

32

33

THE FOUR SEASONS

35

34

37

36

38

39

41

42

SEA PALMS

On Georgia's St. Simons Island

43

34. WSBC, a Chicago radio station. Designed in 1966 by Herbert Pinzke. **35.** The Four Seasons, a restaurant. Designed in 1959 by Emil Antonucci. **36.** Travel Lodge, a motel chain. Has long used the "Sleepy Bear" trademark. Now it has special family rates accompanied by Sleepy Bear Club membership cards, hand puppets, rings, T-shirts, etc. **37.** Oasis Restaurants, of the Illinois Tollway Authority. Designed in 1971 by Morton Goldsholl & John Weber. **38.** Cowardly Lion Stables, Inc., trotting-horse owners. Corporate identity program which included jockey silks, horse blankets, stationery. Designed in 1973 by May Bender. **39.** Fisher Marine, manufacturer of boating supplies. **40.** Saratoga Performing Arts Center, Summer Festival, 1973. Designed by Halprin, Williams & Associates, Inc. **41.** Playboy Club, Inc. Bunny symbol for the clubs and "Playboy" magazine. Designed in 1953 by Arthur Paul, V.P. and Art Director. **42.** The Compound, a restaurant. Designed by Alexander Giraard. **43.** Sea Palms, a resort community, inn and conference center, created by Evans & Mitchell Industries. Designed in 1971 by Creative Services of Atlanta. **44.** Coconut Grove Hotel. Sailboats and palm trees. Designed in 1973 by Murray Gaby of Barrett & Gaby, Inc.

44

45. The Public Trust Theatre Company, a film theater. Designed by William Bogusky of The Brothers Bogusky. **46.** "The Two of Us," a Cinema V film. Designed by Saul Bass & Associates, Inc. **47.** Duck Key, a resort in the Florida Keys. Has since changed its name to Indies House. Designed in 1962 by The Brothers Bogusky. **48.** Outboard Marine Corporation. Stylized sea horse. Designed in 1958 by Dave Chapman & Associates. **49.** Coronado Yachts, a division of Whittaker Corporation. Conquistador symbol is used on sails as well as in conventional ways. Developed in conjunction with the company's ad agency, Charles Mottle & Co. **50.** "The Pentagon Papers," produced by American Documentary Films. Title and trademark designed by Saul Bass & Associates, Inc. **51.** WPBT, Channel 2, Public Television, North Miami, Fla. Designed by Charles Hamilton, the station's Art Director. **52.** Pittsburgh Zoological Society. 1972. **53.** & **54.** Pedal Stuff, clothing and accessory line, a division of Columbus Cycle & Supply Co. Trademark (53) designed in 1972 by Janet R. Bangston and Mike Wendelken. 54 is a patch adaptation by Peter J. Knight.

48

49

50

51

52

53

54

56

57

58

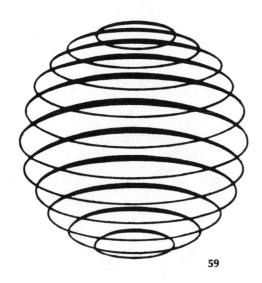

59

55. Marco Polo Club, a Hilton restaurant at the New York World's Fair, 1964–65. Used on menus, flatware, dinnerware, etc. Designed by May Bender of Lane-Bender, Inc. **56.** Slazenger, manufacturer of sports equipment. **57.** Landmark Hotel & Casino. Designed in 1967 by Dickens Design Group. **58.** Philadelphia Flyers, N.H.L. Designed in 1969 by Mel Richman, Inc. **59.** Hemisphere Club, Restaurant Associates. Designed by George Nelson & Co., Inc. **60.** The Bishop's Lodge, ranch resort. **61.** America House Motor Inns, Inc., a division of Richmond Hotels, Inc. **62.** Felix Neck Wildlife Trust. Designed by Anne Hale. **63.** Hersheypark, Hershey, Pa. Symbol derived from local "hex" signs, with each whorl a different bright color. Designed in 1972 by Bofinger-Kaplan. **64.** Horatio's, a restaurant. Named after Capt. Horatio Hornblower. Designed in 1973 by Murray Gaby of Barrett & Gaby, Inc. **65.** Brian Piccolo Cancer Research Fund, an annual fund-raising golf day featuring stars of the National Football League playing golf with the contributors. Used on all promotional paper and materials, souvenirs, trophies. Designed in 1973 by Emil M. Cohen.

THE BISHOP'S LODGE

60

61

62

63

64

65

66

67

68

SECONDS

69

70

66. Channels 8 & 9, closed-circuit television in Miami. Designed in 1963 by The Brothers Bogusky. 67. PBS, Public Broadcasting Service, network for 205 noncommercial TV stations. Logotype designed by Ernie Smith of Lubalin, Smith, Carnase, Inc., under direction of Lawrence K. Grossman, Inc., advertising agency for PBS. 68. Antilles Yachting Service. The "a" forms the boat. Designed by Selame Design Associates. 69. "Seconds," a John Frankenheimer film. Designed by Saul Bass of Saul Bass & Associates, Inc. 70. Philadelphia National League Club. Patch designed in 1969 by deMartin-Marona & Associates, Inc. 71. WMYQ-FM, radio station in Miami. Designed in 1972 by The Brothers Bogusky. 72. "Goat's Head Soup," trademark for record album by The Rolling Stones. 73. Sea Craft, boat builders. Suggests propeller motion and water. Designed in 1973 by Barrett & Gaby, Inc. 74. Office of the Commissioner of Baseball. Major League "Baseball Bannermark," not intended for commercial use. Designed in 1970 by deMartin-Marona & Associates, Inc. 75. Jai-Alai, a pelota court. This logo uses the pelota for the J, the ball for both design and a dot over the I. Designed by Bud Jarrin of New York for Milton Roth, the Coral Gables agency.

71

TM

72

73

baseball

74

JAI·ALAI

75

THE CHICAGO BEARS

76

ALBERT **PICK**
HOTELS · MOTOR INNS

77

78

79

80

Tiffany's Attic
A Dinner Playhouse

81

HOWARD JOHNSON'S

82

Bancroft

83

84

tm

85

HR

86

▌▌▌▌

Spectrum

87

76. The Chicago Bears, a football club. Proposed new mark. Designed in 1973 by Emil M. Cohen. **77.** Albert Pick Hotels & Motor Inns. Designed in 1961. **78.** Indoor Tennis Club. Designed in 1972 by Goldsmith, Yamasaki & Specht, Inc. **79.** The Mutiny at Sailboat Bay, a private club. Designed by Jerry Fand. **80.** Navigator Restaurant. Design by DeStasio, 1951, based on a sculpture at the New Bedford Whaling Museum. **81.** Tiffany's Attic. Designed in 1972 by John Quastler Associates, Inc. **82.** Howard Johnson's inns, hotels and restaurants. Designed by Gianninoto Associates, Inc. **83.** Bancroft Sporting Goods Company. Designed in 1971 by Alan Halladay. **84.** World Famous, a division of American Recreation Group, manufacturer of sporting, camping and recreational equipment. Designed in 1973 by deMartin-Marona & Associates, Inc. **85.** Kreeger & Son, camping gear. **86.** Hubbell Robinson, a film production company. Designed in 1960 by Gould & Associates, Inc. **87.** Spectrum, a Philadelphia sports arena. Designed in 1970 by Mel Richman, Inc.

CIVIC INSTITUTIONS AND EDUCATION

There are no venerable trademarks in this section—symbolization of public services and institutions is a relatively new concept. A community college founded as recently as 1964 traded in its "traditional" seal in 1970 for a new mark combining a letter form with a schoolhouse abstraction—an updated, simplified device. The symbol for the International Women's Year (Fig. 92) is endlessly—even dotingly—employed because it is a simple strong design with an effective interplay between two themes: the inner design of the biological symbol and the outer form of the peace dove. Many of the best marks gain their wit and strength from the use of visual-illusion devices, as in Fig. 111, where the child's head is merely part of the mother's silhouette; the observer completes the illustration from his own life experience.

These trademarks are employed to increase public awareness of the work of the institution and for promotional drives for personnel and funds. Employed in advertising, directional signage, direct mail and television, and on bumper stickers, pins and shirts, they must be memorable, unique and suitable for today's life styles.

88

89

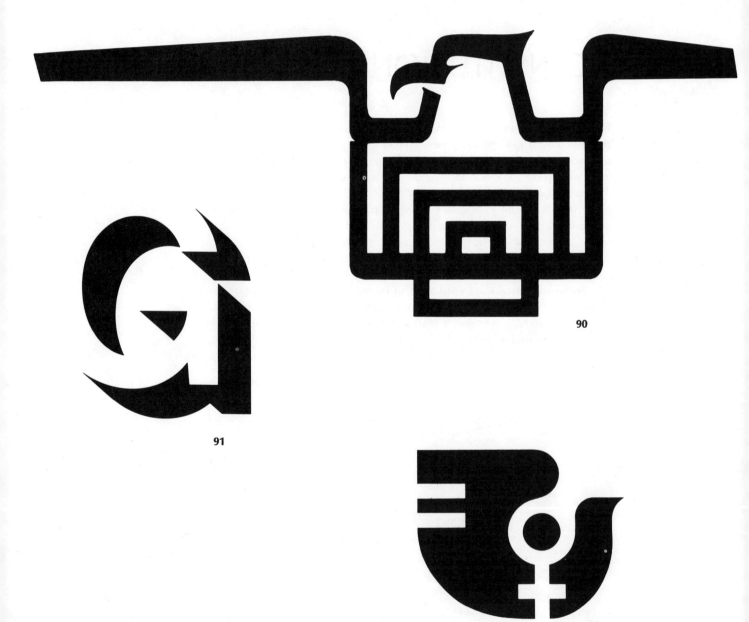

90

91

92

88. Annenberg Center, a research facility for the performing arts in Philadelphia. Designed in 1972 by KMLG (Kramer, Miller, Lomden, Glassman). **89.** Philadelphia. Trademark used by Sept. 1973 Philadelphia Forum for Chartered Life Underwriters. Designed by Frank Nofer, Inc. **90.** John F. Kennedy Center for the Performing Arts, Washington, D.C. Designed in 1972 by Sy Friedman Associates, Inc. **91.** Geisinger Medical Center. Designed in 1973 by Peter Muller-Munk Associates, Inc. **92.** International Women's Year. The official emblem of the UN General Assembly for 1975 represents a stylized dove, the biological symbol for woman and the mathematical sign for equality. Designed by Valerie Pettis, Boston. **93.** New York Merchandise Mart. Designed in 1972 by Sy Friedman Associates, Inc. **94.** Wakamatsu Colony Centennial, Japanese American Citizens League, 1969. Commemorative seal by Aizawa Associates. **95.** Peace Corps. Designed in 1967 by Morton Goldsholl of Goldsholl Associates. **96.** Stadium Authority, City of Pittsburgh. Designed in 1967 by Peter Muller-Munk Associates, Inc. **97.** School Construction Research Seminar, Miami, 1964. Designed by The Brothers Bogusky.

98

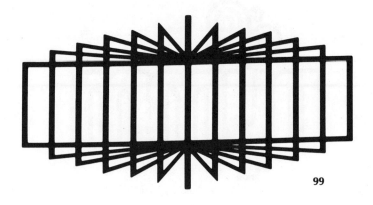

99

100

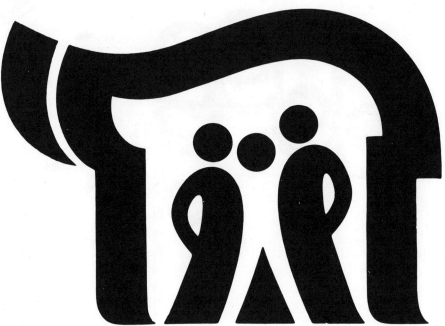

101

102

98. Earthweek, New York City, 1971. Designed for the Council of Environmental Advisors for New York State by Propper–Elman. **99.** Madison Square Garden. Designed in 1969 by Sy Friedman Associates, Inc. **100.** United Fund. Nationally used emblem for community giving in a "united way." Designed by Saul Bass & Associates, Inc. **101.** Jewish Community Center, Miami. The framing shape is a Hebrew word used as an amulet. Designed in 1973 by Barrett & Gaby. **102.** Stamp Out Smog Society, Share a Ride Campaign, Los Angeles. Designed by Saul Bass & Associates, Inc. **103.** Mass Transit Administration, Baltimore. Stylized T. Designed in 1970 by Royal Dadmun & Associates, Inc. **104.** Marathon Jewish Community Center, New York City. Designed by Jack Schecterson & Associates, Inc. **105.** Montessori Family Center, Boston. Designed by Joseph Selame of Selame Design Associates. **106.** First Isaiah Corporation, a religious group in Lower Merion Township, Philadelphia. Designed in 1970 by Mel Richman, Inc. **107.** Pathfinders Fund, a population-control organization. Designed in 1970 by Morton Goldsholl and John Weber of Goldsholl Associates. **108.** The Hartford Civic Center. Designed in 1973 by Peter Muller-Munk Associates, Inc.

103

104

105

106

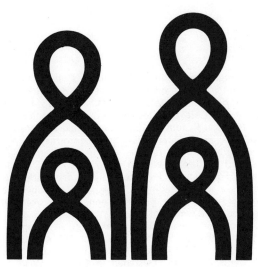

107

108

109

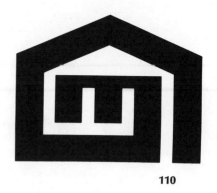

110

111

112

113

109 & 110. Montgomery County Community College, Blue Bell, Pa. 1964 design (109) and new symbol (110) designed in 1970 by Frank Nofer of Frank Nofer, Inc. **111.** Women's Hospital & Maternity Center of Chicago. Designed in 1972 by Michael Reid Design. **112.** National Reading Council. Designed in 1971 by Saul Bass & Associates, Inc. **113.** United States Information Agency, part of the overall design of the exhibit "Industrial Design, U.S.A." Designed by George Nelson & Co., Inc. **114.** The Learning Disabilities Foundation, Inc., remedial work with dyslexia victims. Depicts a figure reading a book. Designed by Gregory Fossella Associates. **115.** Joseph P. Kennedy Physical Fitness Award. Designed by Raymond Loewy / William Snaith, Inc. **116.** Pax Roman, The Academy of Food Marketing, St. Joseph's College. Designed in 1970 by Mel Richman, Inc. **117.** Louisiana Stadium. Designed in 1971 by Peter Muller-Munk Associates, Inc. **118.** Foster Parents Plan, Inc. Designed in 1969 by Wise Advertising Company.

114

115

116

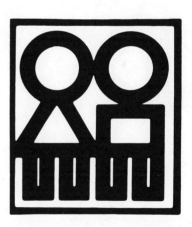

118

117

119

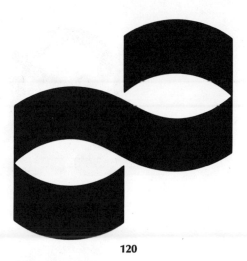

120

121

122

123

119. The Lighthouse for the Blind. Designed in 1965 by Gianninoto Associates, Inc. **120.** San Francisco's Golden Gate Bridge, Highway and Transportation District. Designed in 1970 by Walter Landor Associates. **121.** Norfolk Regional Airport & Botanical Gardens. Designed in 1972 by Peter Muller-Munk Associates, Inc. **122.** Mayor's Office for Volunteers, New York City. Designed in 1970 by Gerstman & Meyers, Inc. **123.** Graduate School of Management, UCLA. Designed by Saul Bass & Associates, Inc. **124.** Irwin Memorial Blood Bank. Designed in 1970 by Walter Landor Associates. **125.** Rehabilitation Institute of Chicago. Designed in 1971 by Morton Goldsholl and John Weber of Goldsholl Associates. **126–128.** Massachusetts Port Authority. Under their new corporate identification program, Boston's transportation facilities are promoting a pay-as-you-go plan. Designed by Gregory Fossella Associates. **129.** Appalachian Adult Basic Education Program, funded by U. S. Office of Education. Mark used to identify facilities and publications. **130.** Wagner College, Staten Island, New York. Abstract view of the Verrazano Narrows Bridge which connects Staten Island with Brooklyn, straddling a W.

125

124

126

127

128

129

130

131

132

133

134

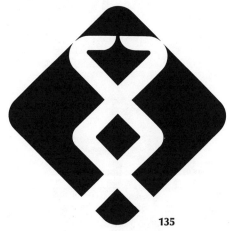

135

136

137

138

139

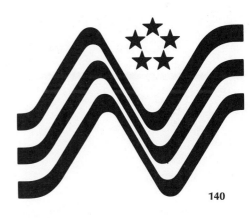

140

141

131 & 132. Goodwill Industries. Old trademark (131) and the new one (132; black and white face on blue ground) designed in 1966 by Selame Design Associates. **133.** New School for Social Research, New York City. Tree symbol designed in 1965 by Burton Wenk of the Wenk Organization. **134.** Pennsylvania Bicentennial. Designed in 1969 by Peter Muller-Munk Associates, Inc. **135.** Medical Professional Building, Miami. Abstract caduceus. Designed in 1970 by Barrett & Gaby. **136.** "Vote 4 Clean Water" Committee, Miami, 1971. Designed by Barrett & Gaby. **137.** Discover America, Inc. Designed by Raymond Loewy / William Snaith, Inc. **138.** The Campaign for Yale. Circle of Y forms as emblem for enormous fund-raising campaign launched in 1975. **139.** Institute for Social Research & Development, Albuquerque, N. M., 1971. **140.** Admiral Nimitz Center, a museum. Designed in 1972 by deMartin-Marona & Associates, Inc. **141.** Better Living Center, New York World's Fair, 1964–65. The design represented six exhibits in a multiple-exhibit building. Designed by May Bender. **142.** Mail Advertising Club, Washington, D.C. Symbol goes with slogan, "The Personal Touch." Designed in 1971 by David Seager of Sanders and Noe.

142

FINANCE, INSURANCE

Many insurance companies and banks and other financial institutions have participated in American visual mythology with their nineteenth-century marks: Prudential's Rock (Figs. 168–70), Metropolitan Life's "The Light that Never Fails" (Fig. 174), the Equitable figure of Justice (Fig. 222), and so forth. But, increasingly, as customers become more sophisticated about finance and as financial firms, competing for business, strive to express efficiency, technological expertise and the power to protect investments and interests, designers have been called upon to abbreviate nomenclature and strengthen and simplify trademarks. This has become one of the strongest areas for new design. Financial institutions are likely to be retail institutions and their graphics must be applicable to signage, whether chastely carved in bronze or looming in illuminated plastic over suburban shopping plazas. Financial marks must also lend themselves to advertising in all media.

INSURANCE COMPANIES

143

144

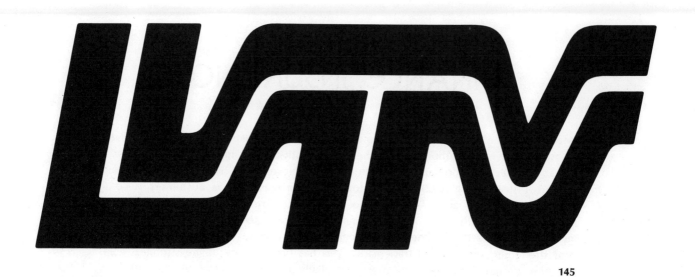

145

146

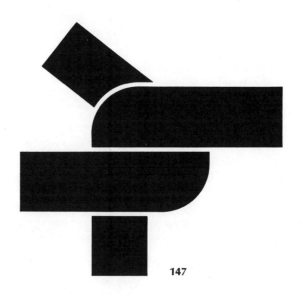

147

NCNB

148

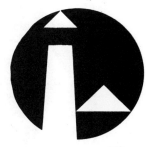

149

150

MB

151

152

143. Reliance Insurance Companies. 144. Continental Bank, Continental Illinois National Bank & Trust Co. Corporate symbol designed in 1969 by Grant / Jacoby; slightly modified in 1972. 145. LTV Corporation (Ling, Temco, Vought, Inc.). Designed in 1972 by Walter Landor Associates. 146. Unity Bank. The merging letter forms symbolize the cooperation of the bank and the Black neighborhood it serves. Designed in 1974 by Gregory Fossella Associates. 147. Lorie Associates, investment broker. Designed in 1972 by The Brothers Bogusky. 148. North Carolina National Bank. Designed in 1973 by Schechter & Luth, Inc. 149. Union Mutual Life Insurance. Designed by Arthur Congdon of Sandgren & Murtha, Inc. 150. State National Bank of El Paso. Designed in 1973 by Walter Landor Associates. 151. Mellon Bank. Designed in 1962 by Peter Muller-Munk Associates, Inc. 152. First National Bancorporation—First of Denver. Designed by Wolfgang Rekow of Lippincott & Margulies, Inc.

153

THE
AMERICA
GROUP

154

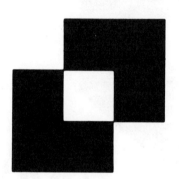

155

156

157

153. Crocker Bank (new shortened name for Crocker-Citizens National Bank). Designed by Peter Graef. 154. The America Group, several life insurance companies. "Official corporate signature" with pilgrim's hat. Designed in 1971 by Cooney & Cooney, Inc. 155. Provident Mutual Life Insurance Co. Designed by Mel Richman, Inc. 156. Oklahoma City's Liberty National Bank & Trust Company. Designed in 1971 by Walter Landor Associates. 157. Marine Midland Bank, New York. Designed by Becker & Becker. 158. Equibank, formerly Western Pennsylvania National Bank. Designed in 1973 by Lefkowith, Inc. 159. American Stock Exchange, Inc. Designed in 1968 by Sandgren & Murtha, Inc. 160. Capital Spectrum, financial consultants. Designed in 1970 by Alan Berni & Associates, Inc. 161. Chase Manhattan Bank. Designed in 1963 by Tom Geismar of Chermayeff & Geismar Associates. 162–165. Phoenix Mutual Life Insurance Company. Rendering of Hartford home office building (162), used since mid-1960s; latest abstract phoenix-and-flame design (163); an early version of the phoenix (164); the phoenix design still used by the Greenfield, Mass., office (165).

Equibank

158

159

CAPITAL SPECTRUM

160

162

163

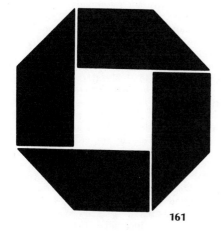

161

164

165

166

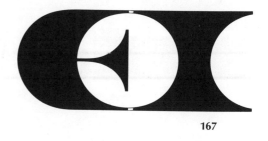

167

168

169

170

171

166. Pittsburgh National Bank. Blue & white. 167. Equitable Life Insurance of Iowa. Designed by Raymond Loewy / William Snaith, Inc. 168–170. Prudential, an insurance company which now deals with a range of plans from group pensions to annuities. Both its famous Rock of Gibraltar and its logo have been updated 1896 version (168); version before 1970 (169); new version (170), designed by Sandgren & Murtha, Inc. 171. Bank of America. Designed in 1969 by Walter Landor Associates. 172. New York Life Insurance Company. In the 1850s the trademark was an eagle feeding its young. In 1954 the mark NYLIC in an oval was adopted. New version shown here was designed in 1964 by Lippincott & Margulies, Inc. 173. Great American Insurance Company. When founded in 1872, the company used the figures of Germania and America. The German imperial eagle was used from the 1880s until 1918, when it gave way to the American eagle. New design (left side red, right wing blue) by Keith N. Thomas. 174 & 175. Metropolitan Life Insurance Co. The famous old tower and slogan (174) were replaced in 1964 with the abstract symbol (175) designed by Don Ervin. 176. First Wisconsin Bancshares Corporation. Designed in 1973 by Walter Landor Associates. 177–179. State Farm Insurance Companies, founded 1922. Modernization (177) 1953 by Whitaker, Guernsey Studio; registered 1956. The emblem had long been a Buick coupe (178). In 1936, the Life & Fire Companies were added to the symbol (179).

172

GREAT AMERICAN INSURANCE COMPANY

173

THE LIGHT
THAT
NEVER FAILS

174

176

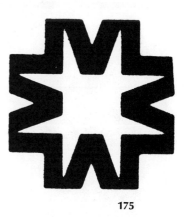

175

STATE FARM

Auto
Life   Fire

INSURANCE ®

177

178

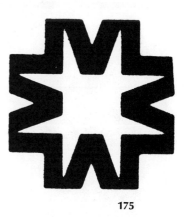

179

180
(1861)

181
(1871)

182
(1904)

183
(1920)

184
(1930)

188
(1971)

185
(1940)

186
(1950)

187
(1960)

189

Alexander
&Alexander

190

191

192

193

180-188. The Hartford, a group of insurance companies. Stag used since 1861. The 1861 version (180) was used on a policy issued to Abraham Lincoln. The 1871 version (181) derived from Sir Edwin Landseer's painting "The Monarch of the Glen." In 1960 Bernard Brussel-Smith did the woodcut adaptation which was revised for the company's contemporary image in 1967 and introduced in 1971 by Sandgren & Murtha, Inc. (188). 189. Banco, Northwest Bancorporation. Designed in 1973 by Schechter & Luth, Inc. 190. Alexander & Alexander, Inc., insurance agents, brokers and consultants. Designed by Wolfgang Rekow of Lippincott & Margulies, Inc. 191. The First National Bank of Fort Worth, Texas, which has shortened its name to The First of Fort Worth. 192. Chase Manhattan Mortgage and Realty Trust. Designed by Edward C. Kozlowski Design, Inc. 193. Escalade, a diversified holding corporation. Designed in 1973 by Alan Berni & Associates, Inc. 194. Savings Bank Association of New York State. Designed in 1962 by Francis Blod Design.

194

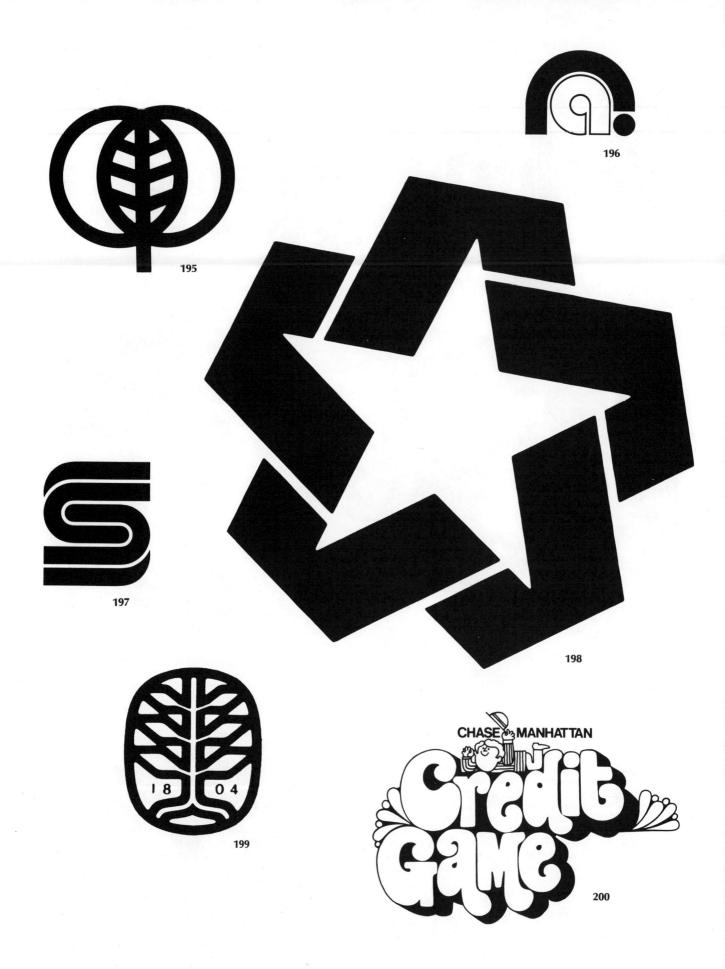

195

196

197

198

199

200

201

202

New Hampshire Insurance Group 1869

203

204

195. Bank of New Hampshire National Association. Designed in 1969 by Gregory Fossella Associates. 196. International Assurance, Inc. Designed in 1972 by Izhar Zik of Zik Advertising. 197. Security First National Bank, California. Designed by Saul Bass & Associates, Inc. 198. First American National Bank, several small banks throughout Tennessee and national financial services. Designed in 1973 by Schechter & Luth, Inc. 199. National Newark & Essex Bank. New symbol for enlarged operations, 1972. 200. Chase Manhattan Bank. Symbol designed for an exhibit in 1971 by Gerstman & Meyers, Inc. Also used on collateral material. 201. CIT National Bank of North America, an affiliate of CIT Financial Corporation. 202. First National Bank of Louisville. Designed in 1973 by Walter Landor Associates. 203. New Hampshire Insurance Company. The "Old Man of the Mountain" has been used as a trademark since 1870. The present-day logo was designed in 1964, using the irregular back of the Old Man's head, by Laurence C. Hall; changed slightly in 1970. 204. Wells Fargo Bank. The trademark reflects the firm's Western past since 1852. Symbol is no longer used for all advertising purposes. Designed in 1973 by Walter Landor Associates. 205. United Banks of Colorado. The chain motif symbolizes the chain of banks along the Rocky Mountains. Designed by Bruce Blackburn of Chermayeff & Geismar.

205

206

207

208

209

211

210

206. Harris Trust and Savings Bank. Designed in 1973 by Schechter & Luth, Inc. **207.** Aetna Life & Casualty. Designed by Lippincott & Margulies, Inc. **208.** Allstate Insurance Co. The "good hands" symbol, designed in 1951 by the now defunct advertising agency, Goodkind, Joyce & Morgan, is rarely used now. In 1966, it was redesigned by Sandgren & Murtha, Inc. **209.** City Investing. Designed in 1970 by Edwin Lefkowith of Lefkowith, Inc. **210.** Beverly Hills Bank. Designed by Gould & Associates, Inc. **211.** The Devon Group, a real-estate and condominium investment firm. Designed in 1973 by The Brothers Bogusky. **212.** Ocean County National Bank, 1972. **213.** Pan American Bank of Miami. Designed in 1959 by The Brothers Bogusky. **214.** Cleveland Bank & Trust. This C & T by Sandgren & Murtha, Inc., replaced a Tudor-style name which had served 50 years. **215.** Overseas Investors, Inc. Designed in 1973 by Gerstman & Meyers, Inc. **216 & 217.** Merrill Lynch, Pierce, Fenner & Smith, Inc., Investment Banking Division. Concept by Ogilvy & Mather, Inc.; illustration of herd (216) by Martella, 1973. Logo (217) designed by the late Lester Beall.

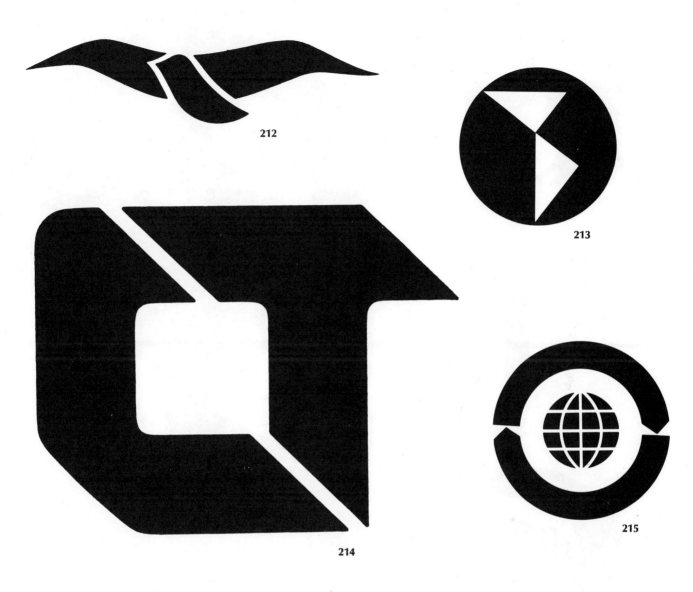

212

213

214

215

216

217

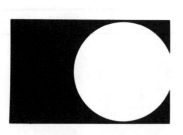

218

219

220

221

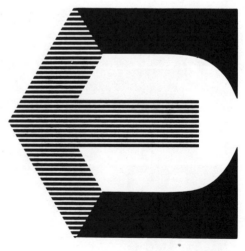

223

The EQUITABLE Life

222

218. Chubb Corporation. Designed by Raymond Loewy / William Snaith, Inc. 219. Citizens Fidelity Bank & Trust Company. The C and F form a tree. Designed by Gianninoto Associates, Inc. 220. Family Funding, Inc. Designed in 1969, when the company was new, by Selame Design Associates. 221. Commonwealth Life Insurance. Designed by Gianninoto Associates, Inc. 222. The Equitable Life Assurance Society of the United States. The figure of "Protection" was introduced in 1963. The final version was done by several men, among them the sculptors Henry Kreis and Paul Fjelde and the painters Robert Riger, Eugene Karlin and John Morning. 223. Unigard Insurance Group. Designed in 1969 by Walter Landor Associates. 224. The Peoples' Trust & Savings Company, Fort Wayne, Indiana. Designed by George Nelson & Co., Inc. 225. Ventures Research & Development Group. Designed in 1970 by Mel Richman, Inc. 226. International Marketing Organization, consultants on U.S.-European real estate, no longer operative. Designed in 1966 by The Brothers Bogusky. 227. Travelers Insurance. "Red Umbrella" adopted in 1959. Since then, ribs and tips were eliminated and initial T removed from hood. In 1970, enclosed in black outline square. 228. Rockefeller Industries. Designed 1968–1971 by Sy Friedman Associates, Inc. 229. Wilmington Savings Fund Bank. The mark symbolizes sheltered growth for customers' savings. Designed by Raymond Loewy / William Snaith, Inc.

FOODS AND BEVERAGES

The enormous franchise and marketing problems involved in altering an old brand-mark in this area lead to great care being taken before a mark is changed. This is particularly true when the symbol is a trade figure, like one-eyed Mr. Boh (Fig. 235), who was seen by generations of beer drinkers as a lovable character, capable of making human errors. Such subjective projections attach to the Underwood devil (Figs. 246–47), the Jolly Green Giant (Figs. 278–80), the Campbell kids (Fig. 288), the Morton Salt girl (Figs. 323–24), Borden's Elsie (Fig. 277) and many others. Such was—and is—the power of the trade figure to evoke positive associations for the company, that Quaker, now a giant conglomerate, decided to update, rather than retire, its kindly Quakers Oats figure (Figs. 254–56). But even nonrepresentational trademarks associated with older brands must also be changed cautiously in order to protect franchises, as the sequence of Pepsi-Cola illustrations shows (Figs. 299–305).

Small details often impress themselves strongly upon consumer consciousness. Thus, the pineapple-crown-shaped accent over the o in Dole (Fig. 287) becomes an important marketing device for the manufacturer. The many shields, crests and heraldic designs used in beverage and food trademarks are, of course, meant to imply quality and reliability. The cartouches used by Del Monte (Fig. 289) and Beatrice Foods (Fig. 259) derive from historic architecture, and are also used primarily for their quality associations. However, these design elements also offer a natural and convenient way of setting the corporate trademark apart when used in packaging or advertising.

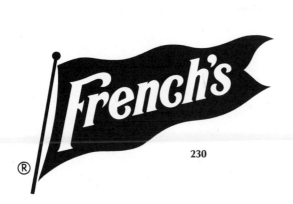

230

231

232

233

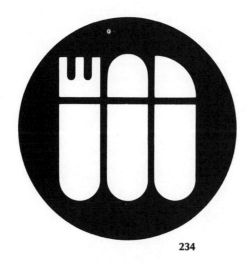

234

230. R. T. French Company. Design used since 1915. The original pennant was much more elongated. **231.** Bell Brand Foods. Designed in 1963 by Gianninoto Associates, Inc. **232.** Burry's, a division of the Quaker Oats Company. This figure, for Mr. Chips chocolate chip cookies, dramatized the concept that Burry's was using "more chips." Designed by Sandgren & Murtha, Inc. **233.** Fairmont Foods. Designed in 1970 by Morton Goldsholl and John Weber of Goldsholl Associates. **234.** Matlaws Food Products. Designed in 1971 by Gregory Fossella Associates. **235.** National Brewing Company's National Bohemian Beer. The "Mr. Boh" trade figure. **236.** Canada Dry, currently Canada Dry Corporation. Designed in 1958 by Raymond Loewy Design Associates. The map, without shield and crown, was originally used in 1903. **237.** Armour & Company. Designed in 1968 by Walter Landor Associates. **238.** General Foods Corporation. Corporate seal designed in 1962 by Walter Dorwin Teague Associates, Inc. **239.** Sealtest Dairies. Designed by Raymond Loewy / William Snaith, Inc. **240.** Blumenthal Bros. Chocolate Company. Designed in 1956 by Gianninoto Associates, Inc. **241.** Good Humor, a division of Thomas J. Lipton, Inc. Designed in 1963 by Gianninoto Associates, Inc.

235

236

237

238

239

240

241

wagner

242

Colonial

243

245

244

246

247

248

249

250

251

242. Wagner Industries, Inc. Designed in 1967 by Dickens Design Group. 243 & 244. Colonial Provision Company. Old pilgrim trademark (243) designed by Chirurg & Cairns, Inc. New pilgrim (244) designed in 1972 by Joseph Selame of Selame Design Associates. 245. Vita Food Products, Brown & Williamson Company. Designed in 1969 by Gould & Associates, Inc. 246 & 247. William Underwood Company. The old "Red Devil" trade figure (246) was first used in 1870. Modernized (247) in 1968 by Robert G. Neubauer, Inc. 248. Fifth Season, McCormick & Company, Inc. Designed in 1970 by Gianninoto Associates, Inc. 249. Arabread. Designed by Selame Design Associates. 250. Anheuser-Busch, Inc. Corporate symbol. 251. Old London Foods, Inc., a division of Borden's. Originally designed in the late 1950s by Egmont Ahrens. Completely revised and redesigned by May Bender of Lane-Bender, Inc. 252. Elmhurst Milk & Cream Company. Designed in 1972 by Schechter & Luth, Inc.

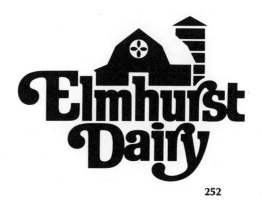

252

253

QUAKER

254

255

256

253. Walter Baker Chocolate, a division of General Foods. "La Belle Chocolatière," a picture by the Swiss artist Jean-Etienne Liotard, was first used in the advertising in 1862 by the company's founder, Walter Baker. The Postum Company, which acquired the firm in 1927, became General Foods in 1929. **254–256.** Quaker Oats Company. Corporate symbol (254) abstracted from original Quaker Oats trademark figure in 1971 by Saul Bass & Associates. It can now be used for a wide variety of products.

TO·RICOS

257

258

BEATRICE

259

260

Parker's

261

262

263

264

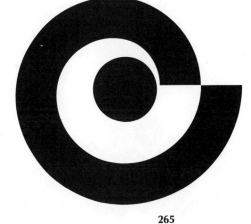

265

266

257. To-Ricos, a division of Con Agra, Inc., marketing Puerto Rican-bred chicken locally. Designed in 1972 by Dickens Design Group. 258. William Frihofer Baking Company. Baker's shovel trademark, designed in 1969 by Mel Richman, Inc. 259. Beatrice Foods Company. Corporate symbol. 260. Central Soya. Designed originally in 1960, revised in 1970 by Lippincott & Margulies, Inc. 261. Parker's. Gaily colored green, orange and red (center circle). Designed in 1965 by Selame Design Associates. 262. Wise Foods, a division of Borden Foods. Designed in 1960 by Jim Nash Associates. 263. Theo. Hamm Brewing Company. Used 1955–1969. Designed by Dickens Design Group. 264. New England Farms, a Maine potato product. Designed by Selame Design Associates. 265. Consolidated Foods Corporation. Designed in 1971 by Walter Landor Associates. 266. Holiday Delight Baking Company. Designed in 1965 by Morton Goldsholl and John Weber of Goldsholl Associates. 267. Pillsbury Company. Corporate trademark replacing the barrelhead with four X's.

267

268

269

CLARK

270

CHOCOLATE HOUSE

272

271

273

268. Foremost Dairies, now Foremost McKesson. Designed in 1959 by Gianninoto Associates, Inc. **269.** Blatz Brewing Company. Designed in 1950 by Dickens Design Group. **270.** Clark Gum Company. Designed and implemented in 1969 by Walter Landor Associates. **271.** P. J. Ritter, a division of Curtice-Burns. Designed by Gianninoto Associates, Inc. **272.** Chocolate House. Used on packaging and in stores. Designed in 1967 by May Bender. **273.** La Choy, a division of Beatrice Foods. Designed in 1968 by Gianninoto Associates, Inc. **274.** Cloverland Dairies, Inc. Designed in 1970 by Royal Dadmun & Associates, Inc. **275.** Danelli Foods. Designed in 1969 by Mel Richman, Inc. **276.** Maxwell House. The famous coffee cup and drop are based on Theodore Roosevelt's tasting the brand and saying "It's good to the last drop." **277.** Elsie-Borden's. Designed in 1954 by Gianninoto Associates, Inc. **278–280.** Green Giant Company. The Jolly Green Giant trademark was originally not green or very jolly. This 1926-1929 version (278) was the birth of an idea, but bears slight resemblance to the latter-day versions. The artist, Jack Baker, was with the LeSueur Company. The modernized version, created in 1960 (279), was the first to echo the now famous "Ho! Ho! Ho!" A trim, handsome Jolly Green Giant, he was used until 1970. The "Giant of the 70s" (280), designed by Lippincott & Margulies, Inc., is rugged . . . more of a "Giant."

Cloverland

274

275

MAXWELL HOUSE ®

GOOD TO THE LAST DROP ℝ

276

ELSIE

277

278

279

280

282

281

283

284

285

286

287

288

290

289

291

281. Petri Wine Company. Designed in 1967 by Gianninoto Associates, Inc. 282. Corporate symbol for the Hunt Wesson Foods division of Hunt Foods & Industries (Wesson Oil and Ohio Matches are in this division). Designed by Saul Bass & Associates. 283. Brach Candy Company. Designed in 1967 by Morton Goldsholl of Goldsholl Associates. 284. Valley Maid Potato Chip Company. Designed in 1971 by Mel Richman, Inc. 285. Royal Crown. Designed in 1965 by Royal Dadmun & Associates, Inc. 286. Log Cabin Syrup, a brand of General Foods. Trademark, intended to honor Lincoln, was designed in 1887 and registered in 1897. 287. Dole. Designed in 1957 by Gianninoto Associates, Inc. 288. Campbell Soup Company. Created by Grace Wiederstein in 1900, the Campbell Kids have since been modified by Roy Williams, Corinne Pauli, Dorothy Jones and the studios of Paul Fennell, Johnstone & Cushing and Mel Richman. 289. Del Monte Corporation. Designed and implemented in 1963 by Walter Landor Associates. 290. Diamond Crystal Salt Company. Designed in 1956 by Dickens Design Group. 291. Austin's Biscuit Company, a division of Fairmont Foods Company. Designed in 1965 by Royal Dadmun & Associates, Inc. 292. Progresso Foods Corporation. Corporate trademark, designed in 1970 by deMartin-Marona & Associates, Inc.

PROGRESSO FOODS CORPORATION

292

293

294

295

297

296

298

(1898)

299

(1905)

300

(1906)

301

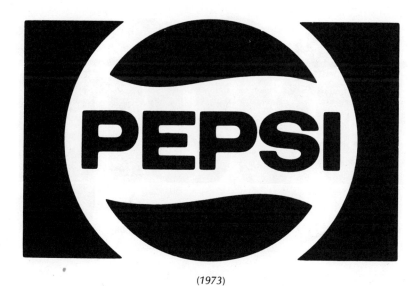

(1973)

305

(1950)

302

(1962)

303

(1969)

304

293 & 294. Loft's Candy, a division of Southland. Old trademark (293) by Edward Russell, 1947. New design (294) by Alan Peckolick, 1973. **295.** Joyva Corporation. Designed by Jack Schecterson & Associates, Inc. **296.** Southland Dairy Division. Corporate trademark, designed in 1967 by Gianninoto Associates, Inc. **297.** Shearer's Dairies, Inc. Designed in 1967 by Mel Richman, Inc. **298.** Sunshine Brewing Company. Designed by Mel Richman, Inc. **299-305.** Pepsi-Cola Company. Current trademark (305) by Gould & Associates, Inc., 1969. The first Pepsi logo (299) was designed by the founder, Caleb D. Bingham, in North Carolina. The latest changes, a square around the circle, repeating the blue and red swaths, are by Frank B. Rupp, Vice President, Graphic Arts.

306

FRITO-LAY

307

LUCKY LEAF

308

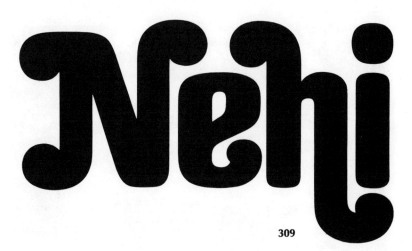

309

KRETCHMER

310

SCHOENER

311

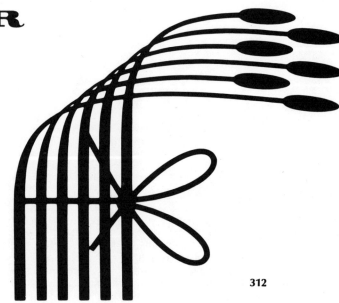

312

313

BROOKS

314

316

315

MR PEANUT
®

317

306. Betty Crocker, a division of General Mills. Adopted in early 1950s. **307.** Frito-Lay, a division of the Pepsi-Cola Company. Designed in 1968 by Royal Dadmun & Associates, Inc. **308.** Knouse Foods, Inc., Lucky Leaf brand. Designed in 1967 by Mel Richman, Inc. **309.** Nehi Beverages, a product of the Royal Crown Cola Company. Designed in 1972 by Gerstman & Meyers, Inc., who aimed at strengthening this brand (a leader in 1924) among young people. **310.** Kretchmer. Designed in 1967 by Gianninoto Associates, Inc. **311.** Schoener Candies, chocolate bunnies and other holiday confections. Designed in 1965 by May Bender. **312.** Foulds Macaroni Company. Designed by Morton Goldsholl and John Weber of Goldsholl Associates. **313.** Buitoni. Designed in 1967 by Gianninoto Associates, Inc. **314.** Brooks Foods, Inc., a subsidiary of Curtice-Burns, Inc. Designed in 1966 by Royal Dadmun & Associates, Inc. **315.** Libby, McNeil & Libby. Designed in 1970 by Gould & Associates, Inc. **316.** Ralston Purina. The checkerboard symbol was created by the founder, William H. Danforth, in 1894. **317.** Planters Peanuts, Standard Brands. "Mr. Peanut," first used in 1916.

SÜPREME

Kitchen Rich

318

319

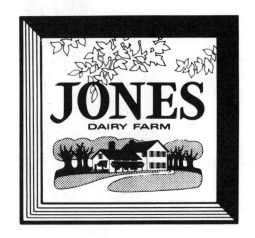

320

BIRDS EYE
REG U S PAT OFF

321

LAND O LAKES

322

324

323

325

318. United Biscuit Company's Supreme Crackers. Designed in 1960 by Morton Goldsholl of Goldsholl Associates. **319.** Paul Masson, a division of Brown-Vintners. Designed in 1959 by Gould & Associates, Inc. **320.** Jones Dairy Farm. Corporate trademark, designed in 1960 by Sidney Dickens. **321.** Birds Eye, formerly a division of General Foods. The trademark, last changed in 1971, is not too different from that on the first "frosted" food packages in 1930, developed by Clarence Birdseye. **322.** Land O Lakes, Inc. The firm was incorporated in 1921 as the Minnesota Co-operative Creameries Association, but changed its name in 1924 after a contest which drew 100,000 entries. The Indian maiden trademark, also created in 1923, was chosen because the lakes region of Minnesota and Wisconsin were the haunts of Hiawatha and Minnehaha. She has only been changed slightly over the years. **323 & 324.** Morton Salt Company. The Morton Salt girl (323) was originated by N. W. Ayer & Co., Chicago, in 1914, with the slogan "When it rains it pours." It was revised (324) in 1966 by deMartin-Marona & Associates, Inc. **325.** Barricini Candies. Designed in 1972 by Art Accardi.

326

327

328

329

330

General Mills

331

332

326. National Biscuit Company (Nabisco). Designed by Raymond Loewy, now Raymond Loewy / William Snaith, Inc. **327 & 328.** Adolph Coors. Still in use, the seal and trademark (327), with a picture of South Table Mountain and a "C," date back to the turn of the century (328). **329 & 330.** Whitman's Chocolates, a division of Pet, Inc. The "Messenger Boy," trademarked since 1921, was modernized slightly in 1958. The "Sampler" concept was originated by then president Stephen E. Whitman, from his wife's stitchery design. **331.** General Mills Corporation. Corporate mark designed in 1962. **332.** Brown Forman Distillers Corporation. Designed by Raymond Loewy.

FURNITURE, APPLIANCES, APPAREL, TEXTILES

Some of the most fascinating stories of trademark history may be found in this group. As in the previous section, many of these marks are trade figures: Buster Brown (Fig. 381), created by a shoe manufacturer and distributor who built a business around this comic-strip cult; the Springmaid girl (Figs. 354–55); the West Point Pepperell griffin (Fig. 348). In housewares, the most familiar older trademarks are not representational, but tend to be letter forms and logotypes: O'Cedar (Fig. 366), Maytag (Fig. 359) and Chemex (Fig. 373). In textiles, abstractions which lend themselves to animation on TV are most successful; for example, Milliken's ribbed monogram (Fig. 377). The noted marks for furniture and accessories manufacturers are the contemporary classics, also mostly monograms: Herman Miller (Fig. 347), Knoll (Fig. 346), Laverne (Fig. 379). The Mohair Council (Fig. 371) and the cotton associations (Figs. 336 and 340) have taken their direction from the "Woolmark" (Fig. 349), but on the whole the apparel industry has not used imaginative or thoughtfully conceived marks on hang tags, labels, or even in advertising. An aggressively promoted mark that is an exception to the rule is L'eggs (Fig. 368).

PERFECT STORAGE

333

334

BRENTWOOD

335

336

337

338

339

340

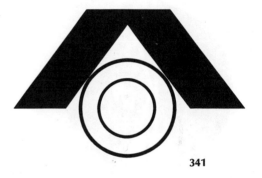

341

342

333. Perfect Storage, refrigerator storage containers. Designed in 1968 by Sy Friedman Associates, Inc., and used until 1970. **334.** Formica Company. Designed by Raymond Loewy / William Snaith, Inc. **335.** Brentwood, housewares. Designed in 1968 by Alan Berni & Associates, Inc. **336.** National Cotton Council of America. Designed in 1971 by Wilbur Mims of Mims Art Associates. **337.** Ellen Tracy, dress manufacturer. Designed in 1972 by Selame Design Associates. **338.** Little Majesty, infants' clothes. Designed in 1966 by Morton Goldsholl and John Weber of Goldsholl Associates. **339.** Storkline Company, infants' furniture. Designed in 1960 by Morton Goldsholl of Goldsholl Associates. **340.** Cotton, Inc., producers division of National Cotton Council. Designed in 1973 by Walter Landor Associates. **341.** American Originals, Oregon and Indiana home furnishings and craft products. Designed in 1964 by Sy Friedman Associates, Inc., and used until 1966. **342.** College Town, Inc. Designed in 1969 by Selame Design Associates.

New from  *Drackett*

344

rosed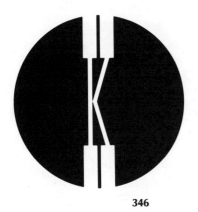le

343

house of
ronnie,inc

345

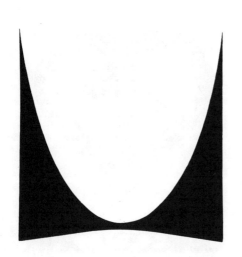

346

343. Rosedale Nurseries, Inc. Designed in 1970 by the staff with the aid of Kenmarc Advertising, Inc. **344.** Drackett Company. Designed by Raymond Loewy / William Snaith, Inc. **345.** House of Ronnie, Inc., girls' and women's apparel manufacturer. Designed by Russell & Hinrichs, Inc. **346.** Knoll International, interior design. Designed in 1948 by Herbert Matter, placed in circle in 1966 by Massimo Vignelli. **347.** Herman Miller, Inc., manufacturers of furniture. Stylized M usually used in red. Designed in 1946 by George Nelson of George Nelson & Co., Inc. **348.** West Point Pepperell, 1965 merger of The West Point Mfg. Co. and the Pepperell Mfg. Co. The griffin is a 1966 redesign of the Pepperell dragon by Lippincott & Margulies, Inc. **349.** International Wool. The woolmark, designed by Francesco Seraglio, is well promoted by the International Wool Secretariat. **350.** Bilnor Manufacturing Company. Designed in 1972 by Robert I. Goldberg Associates, a division of Design For Selling, Inc. **351.** D'Azur Products, a women's soft-goods line of Topco Associates, Inc. Designed in 1966 by Mel Richman, Inc.

347

348

349

350

351

352

353

354

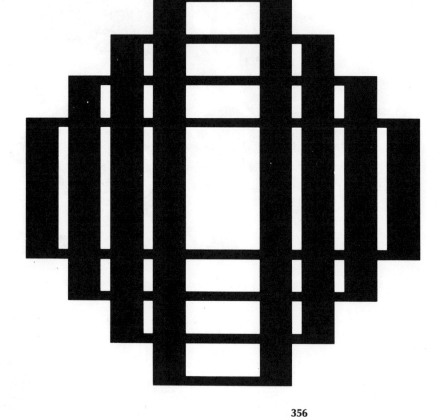

356

® 355

352. Wallace Silversmith, Inc. Designed by Raymond Loewy / William Snaith, Inc. **353.** American Standard, Inc. Designed in 1967 by Peter Muller-Munk Associates, Inc. **354 & 355.** Springs Cotton Mills, "Springmaid." Essentially unchanged in new 1969 version (355) by Royal Dadmun & Associates, Inc., but with clutter removed from background. **356.** Chelsea Industries, textile manufacturers. Designed by Robert A. Gale of Siegel & Gale, Inc. **357.** St. Mary's, a division of Fieldcrest, Inc. Designed in 1970 by Gould & Associates, Inc. **358.** Beauknit Textiles, a division of Beauknit Corporation. **359.** Maytag. White M on blue background, to suggest quality. Designed in 1963 by Chapman, Goldsmith & Yamasaki. **360.** Tyndale Lamps. Designed in 1964 by Sy Friedman Associates, Inc. **361.** Stanley Roberts, stainless flatware and consumer products. Designed in 1965 by Alan Berni & Associates, Inc. **362.** Forum Sportswear. Designed in 1972 by Domsky & Simon.

357

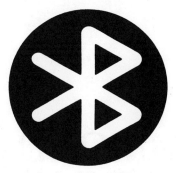

358

359

TYNDALE

360

362

361

HAMMOND
ORGAN

363

364

®

365

366

363. Hammond Organ. One of the first trademarks designed to be reproduced in a four-color process, especially for brochure advertising. Designed by Chapman, Goldsmith & Yamasaki. **364.** Cran Barry, Inc., sports equipment and apparel for women, stressing cheerleading equipment. Designed by Gregory Fossella Associates. **365.** Celanese Corporation. Housemark and accompanying graphic program designed by Saul Bass & Associates, Inc. The bold outer C encloses a more delicate white C. **366.** O'Cedar Company. Designed by Raymond Loewy / William Snaith, Inc. **367.** Sports, Inc., distributors of sporting goods. Designed by Wayland Moore of Wayland Moore Studios. **368.** L'eggs. Hanes Corporation, a product of the Hosiery Division. Designed in 1969 by Lubalin, Smith, Carnase, Inc. **369.** Akro, area throw mats. Designed in 1966 by Alan Berni & Associates, Inc. **370.** Howard Miller Clock Company. Designed by George Nelson & Co., Inc. **371.** Mohair Council of America. Angora goat image designed in 1966. **372.** Talon. The zipper is merely suggested by the dashed-line box, leaving the company free, from an associational viewpoint, to branch into other products. **373.** Chemex Corporation. A coffee-pot shape has been used as trademark since 1948. This mark was designed in 1970 by Arthur Eckstein of Arthur Eckstein & Associates, Inc.

367

368

369

370

Talon®
THE QUALITY ZIPPER

372

MOHAIR

371

373

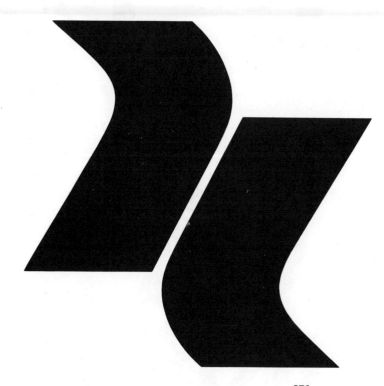

EasyEdges

374

irvinware

375

376

MILLIKEN

377

LEVI'S

378

379

star

380

Buster Brown®

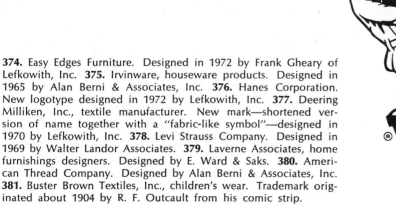

381

374. Easy Edges Furniture. Designed in 1972 by Frank Gheary of Lefkowith, Inc. **375.** Irvinware, houseware products. Designed in 1965 by Alan Berni & Associates, Inc. **376.** Hanes Corporation. New logotype designed in 1972 by Lefkowith, Inc. **377.** Deering Milliken, Inc., textile manufacturer. New mark—shortened version of name together with a "fabric-like symbol"—designed in 1970 by Lefkowith, Inc. **378.** Levi Strauss Company. Designed in 1969 by Walter Landor Associates. **379.** Laverne Associates, home furnishings designers. Designed by E. Ward & Saks. **380.** American Thread Company. Designed by Alan Berni & Associates, Inc. **381.** Buster Brown Textiles, Inc., children's wear. Trademark originated about 1904 by R. F. Outcault from his comic strip.

MISCELLANEOUS CONSUMER PRODUCTS, PAPER PRODUCTS, DRUGS, TOYS

This section covers a wide range of marks, with some relating to large paper-product companies that manufacture many things besides the tissues and paper towels found in every home. Others pertain to dog foods, house paints, tobacco products, toys. The marks are as diverse as the products. In the constant struggle to keep the brand name meaningful, drug companies frequently use trademarks successfully. Even more important can be the trademark for a popular cosmetic, and it is surprising there are not more of them. Perhaps this is because (as with most perfumes, for example) the complete package—its distinctive shape, material, texture, label design, and so forth—is often more important than any of the elements.

383

382

385

386

TRADE   MARK

387

382. Kimberly-Clark Corporation, paper products. Corporate identity symbol designed in 1950 by Dickens Design Group. **383.** Church & Dwight Co., Inc. The "Arm & Hammer," a corporate trademark as well as trademark for baking soda, washing soda and borax brands, was first used by James A. Church in the 1860s when he operated Vulcan Spruce Mills. It represents the arm of Vulcan, who fashioned arms and ornaments for Roman gods and heroes, with hammer about to descend on anvil. In 1867, Church joined his father's baking-soda company and brought the trademark with him. **384.** IBM (International Business Machines). First designed by Paul Rand in 1956. The logotype was supposed to suggest IBM type. **385.** International Paper Company. Combines spruce tree with letter P. Designed by the late Lester Beall. **386.** Armour-Dial, Inc., consumer products. Designed in 1970 by Dickens Design Group. **387.** Smith Brothers Cough Drops, a brand of Warner-Lambert Company. First depicted William Smith ("Trade") and Andrew Smith ("Mark") in connection with their cherry cough candy in 1866 in Poughkeepsie, N.Y. **388.** Cleo, gift-wrapping manufacturers. Designed by Raymond Loewy / William Snaith, Inc. **389.** Crown Zellerbach. Corporate mark is a crowned CZ appearing on all consumer and industrial paper products. Designed by Gianninoto Associates, Inc. **390–392.** Beckett Paper Company. Buckeye trademark developed in 1894. Several intermediate designs led to the current abstract leaf (392) by designer George Tassian. **393.** Edu-mensionals, Inc. Designed in 1970 by Mel Richman, Inc. **394.** Garrett Buchanan, distributors of paper products. 1969.

388

389

392

390

393

391

394

CABLE ADDRESS:
POWHATTAN

396

American Brands Inc.

395

397

398

399

395 & 396. American Brands, Inc. In 1969 the new corporate symbol (395) was developed from the trademark illustration of Powhattan (396), still used by the American Tobacco Company Division. **397.** Incoterm Corporation, manufacturers of desktop computer terminals. Corporate mark developed in 1970 by Donald Deskey Associates, Inc. **398.** Ultima, a Revlon cosmetic treatment line. Designed in 1965 by McFarland Studio, Inc. **399.** Carnival Toy. Trademark designed by Edward C. Kozlowski Design, Inc. **400.** Holliston. Designed in 1968 by Herbert Pinzke. **401.** Speedry, a writing tool. Designed in 1961 by Alan Berni & Associates, Inc. **402.** Ameritone Paint Corporation. Designed in 1970 by Gould & Associates, Inc. **403.** Goldberger Doll Manufacturing Co., Inc. Designed by Jack Schecterson & Associates, Inc. **404.** Aqua Velva, shaving products of the J. B. Williams Company, Inc. Designed in 1955 by Donald Deskey Associates, Inc. **405.** Yardley of London, Inc. Designed in 1962 by Donald Deskey Associates, Inc. **406.** American Can Company. This firm abandoned its old trademark in 1968, when it acquired Northern Paper, Dixie, Marathon and other paper-product firms, and adopted this "action A" suggesting folding and packaging processes, designed by Sandgren & Murtha, Inc.

Holliston
Binding
Fabrics

400

SPEEDRY

401

402

DOLLY & Me

403

AQUA VELVA

404

YARDLEY

405

406

407

Habitat

409

411

410

Lenox

412

407. Bayuk Cigars, Inc., Grand Prix Brand. Designed by Mel Richman, Inc. **408.** Dixie, a division of American Can Company. Designed by Saul Bass & Associates, Inc. **409.** Habitat Education Industries, Inc., infant educational growth products. Designed in 1972 by Sy Friedman Associates, Inc. **410.** Finn Industries, package manufacturers. Designed in 1968 by Sy Friedman Associates, Inc. **411.** Maxikid, by Learning Environment, Inc. Designed in 1970 by Mel Richman, Inc. **412.** Finnaren & Haley, Inc.: Lenox, a regional housepaint. Designed by Mel Richman, Inc. **413.** Carter's Ink, manufacturers of stationery items. Corporate mark developed in 1959 by Donald Deskey Associates, Inc. **414.** Robin Industries, notions manufacturers. Designed in 1968 by The Brothers Bogusky. **415.** J. L. Clark Manufacturing Company, containers. Corporate trademark designed by Herman Bartels of the company in the 1930s. **416.** Hot Spot, miniature welding torch, product trademark designed in 1963 by Sy Friedman Associates, Inc. **417.** United Medical Laboratories. Corporate symbol is "stylized biological cell." Designed by Don Muth, company art director. **418–420.** Sherwin-Williams Company. Trademark (420) (registered in 66 countries) shows paint from can covering the earth, an adaptation of a design (419) sketched by George W. Ford, advertising manager, in 1895. Prior to that, a chameleon (418) mounted on an artist's palette was the trademark.

413

414

416

415

417

418

419

420

421

422

423

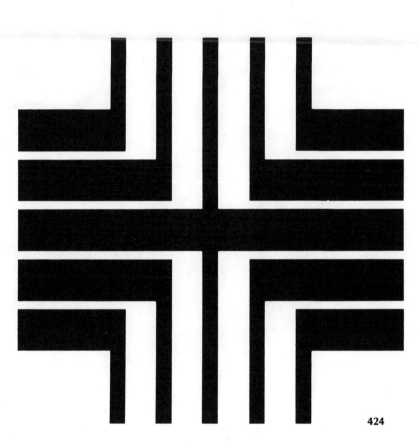

424

425

426

421. Pettit Marine Paint. Tropical fish unchanged since 1956, when mark was originated. **422.** VO-5, Alberto Culver Company, hair-grooming aids. Corporate symbol designed in 1956 by Dickens Design Group. **423.** Statler Tissue Corp. Designed in 1968 by Selame Design Associates. **424.** Pitney Bowes, business systems and equipment. Designed in 1971 by Alan Siegel and Robert A. Gale, in cooperation with Richard K. Jewett, Chairman of the Corporate Identification Committee. New program uses an abstract grid at the center. **425.** Miracle Power Corporation, manufacturers of specialty aerosol lubricants for cars. Corporate mark, with indigo-blue oval and black arrows, designed by Ed Panosian, Collateral Art Division of Baisch, Blake and Gabriel. **426.** Marcal. Designed by Gianninoto Associates, Inc. **427.** Stone Container Corporation. Designed in 1959 by Morton Goldsholl of Goldsholl Associates. **428.** Brown & Williamson. Designed by Gianninoto Associates, Inc. **429.** Eagle Pencil Company. Designed by Raymond Loewy. **430.** Acme, health & beauty-aid products. Designed in 1967 by Alan Berni & Associates, Inc. **431.** Joy Hall's Personal Collection, Ambassador Leather Goods, cosmetics. Designed in 1972 by May Bender. **432.** Martin-Senour Company, paint products. Designed in 1951 by Morton Goldsholl of Goldsholl Associates.

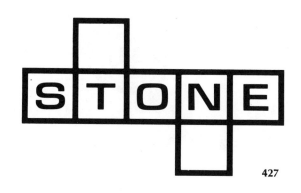

427

428

429

430

431

432

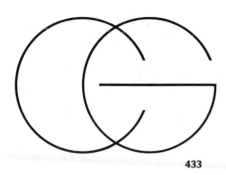

433

PORTER

434

435

436

437

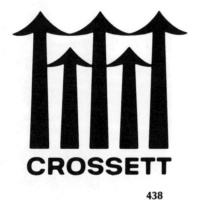

CROSSETT

438

439

88   MISCELLANEOUS CONSUMER PRODUCTS, PAPER PRODUCTS, DRUGS, TOYS

440

441

442

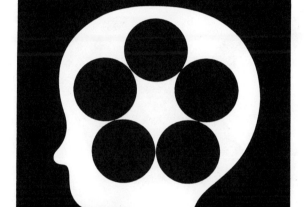

443

444

433. Cover Girl, cosmetics by Noxell Corporation. Trademark designed by Edward C. Kozlowski Design, Inc. **434.** Porter Chemistry Sets. Designed in 1960 by Alan Berni & Associates, Inc. **435.** Container Corporation. Symbol for product-design department. Designed in 1965 by Herbert Pinzke. **436.** Laddie Boy Dog Foods (Lewis Foods, a division of National Can Co.). Designed in 1969 by Gould & Associates, Inc. **437.** Dr. Ross Dog Foods (Lewis Foods). Designed in 1969 by Gould & Associates, Inc. **438.** Crossett Company, paper products. Designed in 1957 by Dickens Design Group. **439.** Rospatch Fabric Tapes, a division of Rospatch Corporation. Designed in 1967 by Peter Muller-Munk Associates, Inc. **440.** Abbott Laboratories. Corporate trademark, a stylized red "a," with application ranging from small pills to multistory building signs. Designed by George Nelson & Co., Inc. **441.** Lundia, filing & storage systems, by Meyers Industries. The bright orange circle is divided by three white bars. **442.** Texize Chemicals, cleaning products. Designed in 1970 by Royal Dadmun & Associates, Inc. **443.** Creative Playthings, Inc. Symbol for the Learning Center, orange-red background with lavender circles in head. Designed by George Nelson & Co., Inc. **444.** Bauer & Black, a division of the Kendall Company, manufacturers of elastic goods. Designed in 1959 by Morton Goldsholl of Goldsholl Associates. **445.** Avery Products Corporation, manufacturer of pressure-sensitive labels. Designed in 1963 by Gould & Associates, Inc.

445

446

Ditto

447

448

449

450

446. Kodak. Trademark for its 34,000 products from tank cars to photographic consumer products. It maintains the corporate colors of red and orange. Designed by Peter Oestreich. 447. Ditto, a division of Bell & Howell, duplicating equipment. Designed in 1958 by Morton Goldsholl of Goldsholl Associates. 448. Packaging Corporation of America. Designed in 1963 by Dickens Design Group. 449. Niemand Industries, Inc., manufacturers of spiral tubing for packaging and electrical equipment. Designed in 1971 by Gerstman & Meyers, Inc. 450. Parkway, "N" gauge electric trains. Designed in 1965 by Sy Friedman Associates, Inc., and used until 1971. 451. Nifty, school products, division of St. Regis Paper Company. Designed in 1964 by deMartin-Marona & Associates, Inc. 452. Tums. Designed in 1965 by Royal Dadmun & Associates, Inc. 453. Healthcare Corporation, medical and dental supplies. Designed in 1969 by Sy Friedman Associates, Inc., but never implemented. 454. Johnson Industries, manufacturer of therapeutic toiletries. Designed in 1967 by Donald Deskey Associates, Inc. 455. Pegasus Luggage. Designed in 1967 by The Brothers Bogusky. 456. Brite Star Manufacturing Company, Christmas decorations. Designed in 1969 by Mel Richman, Inc. 457. Ritz Fragrance, Inc., by Charles of the Ritz. Designed in 1970 by McFarland Studio, Inc.

451

452

453

454

BRITE STAR

456

455

457

458

459

460

461

462

463

458. Parker Adult Games, manufactured by Parker Brothers, Inc. This swirl design by Arnold Arnold was first used in 1964, modified in 1972. **459.** International Minerals & Chemical Corp., insect control. Designed in 1959 by Goldsholl Associates. **460.** Warner Packaging, a division of Rexham, manufacturer of folding cartons, boxes and plastics. Designed by Edward C. Kozlowski Design, Inc. **461.** Weyerhaeuser Company, wood and paper products and containers. First designed in 1959 by Lippincott & Margulies, Inc. The program is under the supervision of Richard E. Lindgren, Manager of Advertising and Communication Programs, and the current materials were developed in coordination with the David Strong Design Group. **462.** Holgate Toy Company, a division of Playskool, Inc. Designed in 1967 by Gianninoto Associates, Inc. **463.** Scott Paper Company. Corporate symbol (blue). Designed by George Nelson & Co., Inc.

RETAILERS

Retailers' trademarks are becoming more significant today. The Brooks Brothers lamb (Fig. 497) is a theme for sedate ties by that store. At the other end of the continuum from this mark, which grew out of the store's history, are the new mass-marketing trademarks, like Zayre's (Fig. 467) or Caldor's (Fig. 482), designed to deflect shoppers on busy highways and to stand out on tightly packed pages of discount advertising and yet add a note of glamor to the packages carried home. Other marks, like those for Ben Franklin (Fig. 477) or Hutzler's (Fig. 479), either refurbish the image of older chains, as in the case of the former, or else help newer suburban stores combat the image of downtown dowager stores, as in the case of the latter.

465

464

466

467

468

Bradlees

469

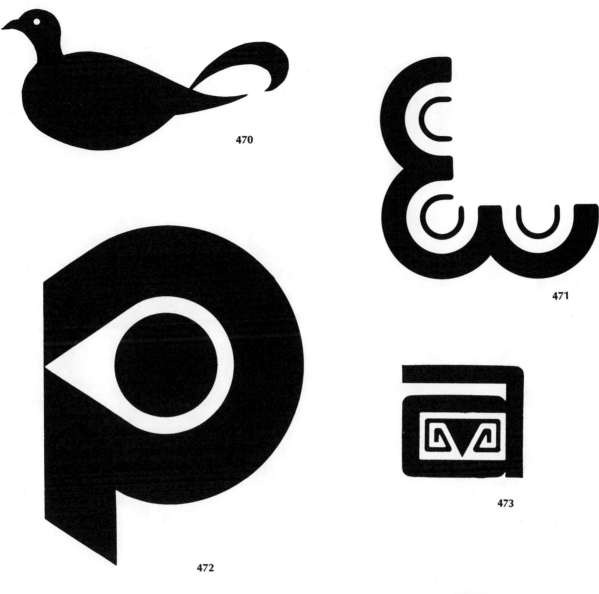

470

471

473

472

464. A & P, The Great Atlantic & Pacific Tea Company, Inc. Symbol registered since 1887. 465. A & W, national chain of root-beer and hot-dog stands. 466. W. & J. Sloane, furniture. Thistle, symbolic of Scottish ancestry of William and John Sloane, first used in 1843. Current version designed in 1958 by the late Andrew Szoeke, outstanding calligrapher. 467. Zayre, discount department store chain. Designed in 1972 by Alan Berni & Associates, Inc. 468. Hills Supermarkets, Inc. Designed in 1968 by Gould & Associates, Inc. 469. Bradlees, discount department store chain. Colors: red, yellow & blue. Designed in 1969 by Joseph Selame of Selame Design Associates. 470. Pampered Chef, Inc. An abstract pheasant for a gourmet "pot shop." Designed by Bunn–Grey. 471. Erica Wilson, needlepoint artist's shop. Designed by Cissy Bruce; consultants, Earth Ink, 1970; revised 1972. 472. Poll Optical Company. Designed in 1968 by Gerstman & Meyers, Inc. 473. Antartex Sheepskin Shops, importers of sheepskin fashions. 474. Kennedy's Food Stores. Designed in 1969 by Selame Design Associates.

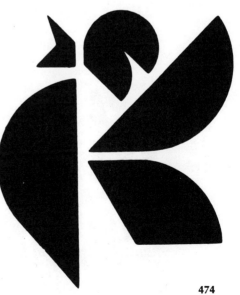

474

MASONS 475

clover
476

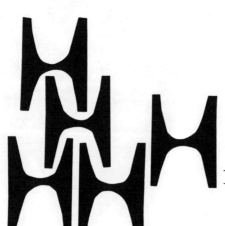

477

478

PENN FRUIT

480

HUTZLER'S
Baltimore

479

Elizabeth Arden ©1971

481

482

483

484

475. Masons Discount Stores, a division of M. H. Fishman Co., Inc. Designed by Jack Schecterson & Associates, Inc. 476. Clover Division, Strawbridge & Clothier department store. Designed by Mel Richman, Inc. 477. Ben Franklin Division, City Products Corporation, variety store. Designed in 1969 by Morton Goldsholl of Goldsholl Associates. 478. Steuben Glass. First designed, by sculptor Sidney Waugh, and used in 1947; registered in 1950. 479. Hutzler Brothers, Inc. This department store chain needed a unifying modern symbol when it reached its 110th year in 1968. Royal Dadmun & Associates, Inc., developed the five stylized H's, representing the company's five stores. Usually used with Hutzler red, the mark is flexible and can be a bouquet of small H's in assorted colors. 480. Penn Fruit Company, grocery chain. Designed by Mel Richman, Inc. 481. Elizabeth Arden. Signature designed by Gene Federico. 482. Caldor, discount department store. Designed in 1972 by Alan Berni & Associates, Inc. 483. Newberrys, discount department store chain. Designed in 1961 by Alan Berni & Associates, Inc. 484. Brigham's Confectionery Shops. Designed in 1964 by Selame Design Associates. 485. Bergdorf Goodman. First designed in 1928 by Kenyon & Eckhardt when this store moved to its present location. Andrew Szoeke later designed the present lettering. 486. Hills Brothers, food supply company. Designed in 1968 by The Brothers Bogusky.

485

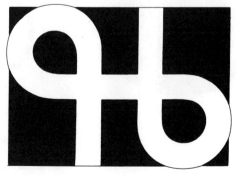

486

487

488

Medi Mart

489

Fun Stop

490

Stop & Shop

491

The Cradle

492

493

the children's place

494

495

Mister
Donut

496

ESTABLISHED 1818   497

498

487. Serigraphix I, fabric retailer. Designed in 1970 by Harry D. McMillan, a partner in the firm. **488.** Foreign Autopart, chain auto-service shop. Designed by Selame Design Associates. **489.** Medi Mart, drugstore chain, one of the Stop & Shop Companies. Designed in 1969 by Selame Design Associates. **490.** Fun Stop, a toy and leisure store chain, one of the Stop & Shop Companies. Designed in 1969 by Selame Design Associates. **491.** Stop & Shop Companies. Corporate symbol, revised in 1973 by Schechter & Luth, Inc. **492.** The Cradle, shop and gallery selling imports. Name and mark concept from early item, wooden cradles for babies and dolls from Hungary and Czechoslovakia. Designed in 1968 by Herbert Pinzke. **493.** The Children's Place, department store chain for children. Designed by George Nelson & Co. **494.** Stop & Shop Companies. Designed in 1963 by Selame Design Associates. **495 & 496.** Mister Donut of America, Inc. New mark (496) designed in 1964 by Selame Design Associates. **497.** Brooks Brothers, clothing. Order of the Golden Fleece, drapers' woolen guild symbol, used by Brooks since the 1850s, patented 1915. **498.** The Meat Man, meat store, 1966–68. Designed by Nancy W. McFarland of McFarland Studio, Inc. **499.** Shultzys, a delicatessen. Designed in 1969 by Selame Design Associates.

499

PRINTING, PUBLISHING AND OTHER SERVICE INDUSTRIES

The firms represented here range from printing and design organizations through management services—some involving new technologies, such as underwater electronics and computer systems—to heavy-labor fields, such as construction and moving. All of these are companies in which the stress is on competence and knowledgeability, and the trademarks reflect this. The exception from the generally rather heavy marks based on monograms, directional lines symbolizing highways, computer input, and so forth, is the area of publishing. Many book publishers' distinctive emblems, called "colophons," derive from fifteenth-century manuscripts; Liveright's symbol (Fig. 510) is typical. Colophons are apt to make direct allusions to literature, as does Viking's (Fig. 523). More recent publications, such as *Avant Garde* (Fig. 547), may depend on hand-lettered logotypes. Designers' personal marks are interesting as examples of the designer on display. We have selected some of the bolder examples, even though there is currently a trend toward understatement. The "chop" of Tamarind Lithography Workshop (Fig. 570) is one of many registered by that firm in an effort to develop personal marks in a manner reminiscent of the way Whistler used his famous butterfly monogram to "sign" his etchings.

500

501

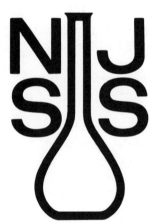

502

503

504

500. Computer Terminal Corp. Designed by Raymond Loewy. 501. Interguide, city-map publisher. Designed in 1965 by The Brothers Bogusky. 502. New Jersey Scientific Supply, Inc. Designed in 1970 by May Bender. 503. Blessing's Corporation, institutional hospital supplies. Designed in 1972 by Alan Berni & Associates, Inc. 504. Graphic Arts Association of Delaware Valley. Designed in 1970 by Mel Richman, Inc. 505. Cardiac Datacoy, Inc., a pacemaker data system whereby all patients using pacemakers are monitored and recharged through computer systems. Designed in 1971 by Mel Richman, Inc. 506. Leo Burnett Co., Inc., advertising agency. Designed by Walter Dorwin Teague Associates, Inc. 507. Hydrotech Corp., underwater electronics. Designed in 1967 by The Brothers Bogusky. 508. SCA Services, national company in the waste service industry. Designed in 1970 by Selame Design Associates. 509. Telautograph Company, electronic longhand delivered in handwritten form. Designed in 1958 by Gould & Associates, Inc.

505

506

507

508

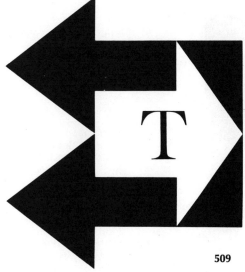

509

510

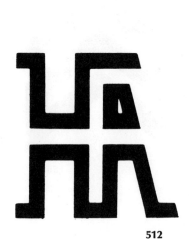

512

513

514

510. Liveright Publishing Corporation. This scholarly monk has long been the firm's trademark. 511. Communications Satellite Corporation. Designed in 1966 by Leslie A. Segal of Corporate Annual Reports, Inc. 512. Hirsch Aarons Design, formerly Pattern Studies, Inc., 1972. 513. Testwell Laboratories, Inc., structural testing for industry, 1970 to present. Designed by Nancy W. McFarland of McFarland Sudio, Inc. 514. Jack Schaffer Typography. Designed in 1969 by The Brothers Bogusky. 515. Meridian Photographs, Inc., printing and processing. Designed in 1965 by Norman Golding of Drawing Board (now out of business). 516. Explosive Technology, a division of Ducommon, Inc. Designed by Saul Bass & Associates, Inc. 517. Information Science, Inc., personnel systems. Designed in 1972 by Dennis Vassilatos, Art Director. 518. H. A. Kyljian & Company, an engineering and architectural firm. Designed in 1971 by Mel Richman, Inc. 519. Canteen, a corporate identity program for Canteen Corporation, a food and vending service. Right wing and lettering are in blue. Designed in 1966 by Dickens Design Group, updated from a 1962 design by Lippincott & Margulies, Inc. 520. Republic Van Lines. Designed in 1971 by Royal Dadmun & Associates, Inc.

515

516

517

518

CANTEEN

519

520

PAX FAX

522

521

523

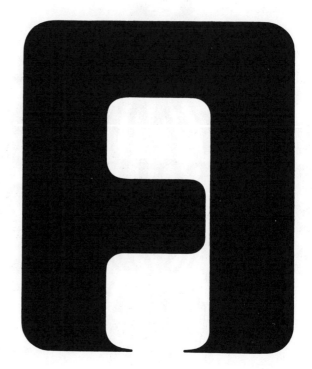

524

525

521. Johnson Paving Co., road builders. Designed by Emil M. Cohen. **522.** Pax Fax, Inc., research laboratories. Corporate identity symbol designed in 1950 by˙Dickens Design Group. **523.** Viking Press, Inc., publishers. **524.** Fine Arts Printing. Designed in 1971 by The Brothers Bogusky. **525.** Araban, institutional supplier. Symbol suggests coffee cups on rotating rack. Designed by Selame Design Associates. **526.** Brown Photo Commercial, photographic processors. Designed in 1970 by Rumsey Lundquist. **527.** International Computer (no longer in business). Designed in 1969 by The Brothers Bogusky. **528.** Interstate United, a moving company. Designed by Chapman, Goldsmith & Yamasaki. **529.** *The New Yorker* magazine's trade figure, Eustace Tilly (named by Corey Ford) or "Mr. New Yorker," by Rea Irwin, used on the first cover in February 1925. **530.** Linen Supply Corporation (no longer in existence). Stacked linen and an L shape. Designed in 1960 by The Brothers Bogusky. **531.** Houghton Mifflin Company, publishers.

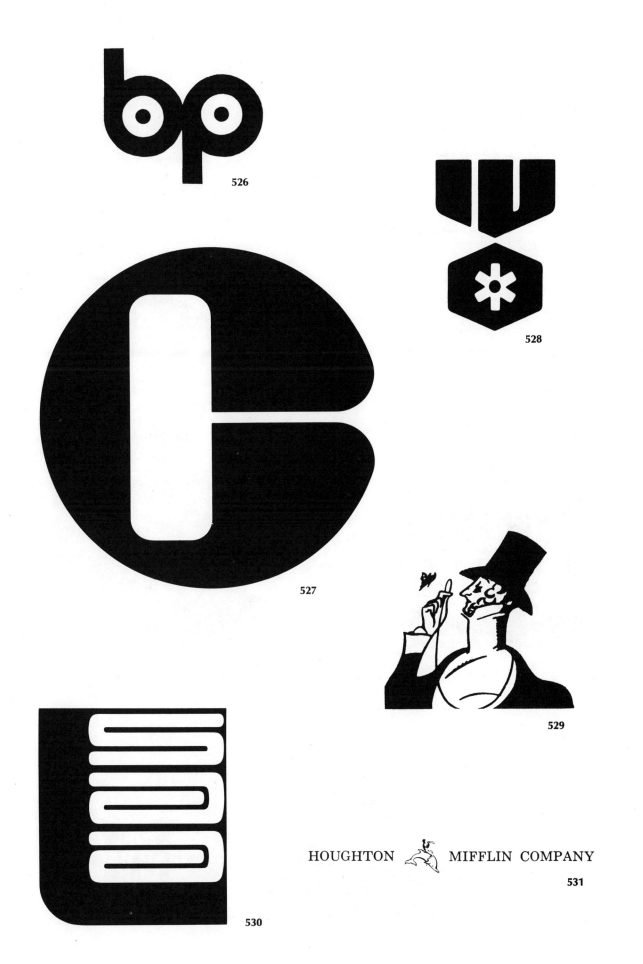

526

528

527

529

HOUGHTON   MIFFLIN COMPANY

531

530

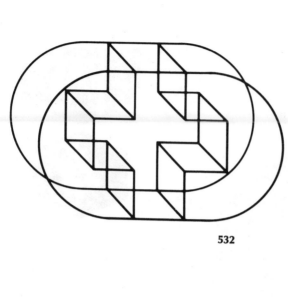

532

533

534

535

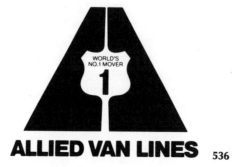

536

537

538

539

540

541

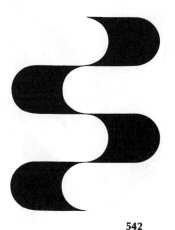

542

532. Curtis & Davis, architects and planners. Designed in 1972 by Peter Muller-Munk Associates, Inc. **533.** Alan Berni & Associates, Inc., marketing consultants and designers. Designed in 1965 by Alan Berni. **534.** William J. Burns International Detective Agency. Designed in 1971 by Howard York Designs. **535.** Supply Line, a division of Ryder Trucking, fast trucking for auto parts. Designed in 1973 by The Brothers Bogusky. **536.** Allied Van Lines. Designed in 1969 by deMartin-Marona & Associates, Inc. **537.** McGraw Hill, Inc., publishers. A new identification program was implemented before a move to new headquarters, marking a "diverse and growing communications complex." The identification standards were developed in 1971 by Sandgren, Murtha, Lubliner, with Ad Tolhuijs creating the symbol, a stacked version of the logo based on a Futura type face. **538.** Peter Press, printers. Reminiscent of Renaissance printer's marks. Designed in 1953 by May Bender of Lane-Bender, Inc. **539.** Chicago Book Clinic, largest professional group promoting craftsmanship in bookmaking. Trademark part of stationery, redesigned in 1968 by Herbert Pinzke. **540.** Transystems, a trucking company. Designed in 1969 by The Brothers Bogusky. **541.** 3-M, a division of Business Publications. Designed in 1969 by Herbert Pinzke. **542.** Diverse Services Corporation, a firm offering management and personnel in the building maintenance field to colleges and universities. Designed in 1972 by Mel Richman, Inc.

THE THOUGHTFUL PEOPLE, INC.

544

543

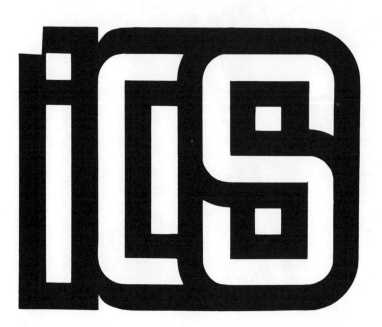

545

546

543. Barksdale Travel Service. Designed in 1971 by Mel Richman, Inc. **544.** The Thoughtful People, Inc., a firm that originates concepts and marketing ideas for new products. Designed by May Bender. **545.** Inter-state Computer Services, Inc. Designed in 1959 by Gerstman & Meyers, Inc. **546.** Booke & Company, public relations and creators of annual reports. Trademark is a play on the name. Designed in 1961 by Gould & Associates, Inc. **547.** Avant Garde magazine. Designed in 1967 by Herb Lubalin. **548.** Color Guild Associates, a national organization of consumer house-paint dealers. Designed in 1971 by Mel Richman, Inc. **549.** E-System, Inc. Designed in 1972 by Walter Landor Associates. **550.** Dukane Corporation, communications systems division. Designed by William H. Goldsmith of Goldsmith, Yamasaki, Specht and Anderson Design, Inc. **551.** Endurance Paving Company, road builders. Designed by Emil M. Cohen. **552.** United Engineers & Constructors, Inc., a subsidiary of Raytheon Company.

110   PRINTING, PUBLISHING AND OTHER SERVICE INDUSTRIES

547

548

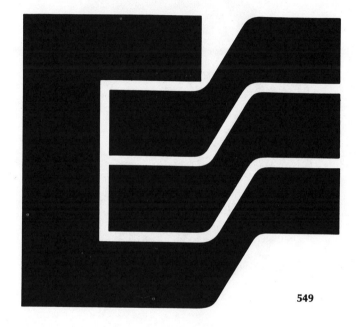

549

550

552

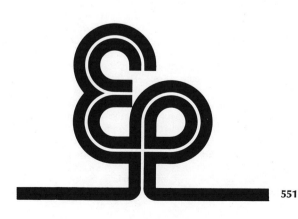

551

553

554

555

556

557

553. E. P. Dutton, publishers. **554.** Geodyne, a division of E. G. & G., an underwater technology company. Designed by Selame Design Associates. **555.** Jeff Cohen, a photographer. Used on his personal stationery and paper. Designed in 1973 by Emil M. Cohen. **556.** Bantam Books, Inc. The original bantam mark appeared in the 1950s. **557.** Hank Gans, photographer. Designed in 1973 by McFarland Studio, Inc. **558.** Dome Laboratories, a division of Miles Laboratories, Inc. Designed in 1973 by Gerstman & Meyers, Inc. **559.** Contamination Reduction Systems, a national environmental systems organization. Designed by Mel Richman, Inc. **560.** Ryder Systems, Inc., a national moving and distribution company. Map of the U.S. inserted in a red R. Designed in 1956–1957 by Design Research, Inc., fully adopted by company in 1970. **561.** Deep Six, underwater salvage company. Designed in 1970 by The Brothers Bogusky. **562.** Area Consultants, Inc., a management consultant firm. Designed by Edward C. Kozlowski Design, Inc. **563.** Manfred Hegeman Associates, design consultants. Designed in 1967 by Manfred Hegeman. **564.** Typographers Association of New York (TANY). Designed in 1969 by Gerstman & Meyers, Inc.

558

559

560

561

562

563

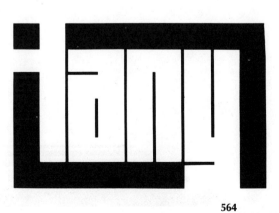

564

566

565

567

568

Calspan

569

570

COMPUTERS
FOR PEOPLE

571

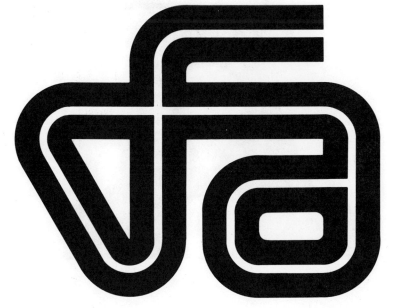

572

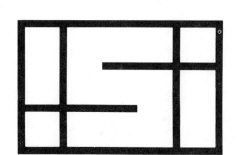

573

565. Raymond Loewy / William Snaith, Inc., industrial designers.
566. Hemingway Transport, Inc., a Northeast regional trucking
company. The symbol reads the same upside down. Designed
in 1972 by Selame Design Associates. **567.** Maison Germaine, a
gourmet catering firm. Designed by Edward C. Kozlowski Design,
Inc. **568.** Capeletti Brothers, road construction. Designed in 1959
by The Brothers Bogusky. **569.** Calspan, formerly Cornell Aero-
nautical Laboratory. Designed in 1972 by Lefkowith, Inc. **570.**
Tamarind Lithography Workshop, Inc. Alchemical symbol. Designed by June Wayne. **571.** Triadex Corp. Designed in 1970 by
Selame Design Associates. **572.** Federal Asphalt Co., manufacturers
of asphalt for road surfaces. Designed in 1973 by Emil M. Cohen.
573. Innovative Sciences, Inc., educational systems for industry.
Designed by Robert A. Gale of Siegel & Gale, Inc. **574.** Saxton
Nuclear Experimental. Designed in 1973 by Mel Richman, Inc.

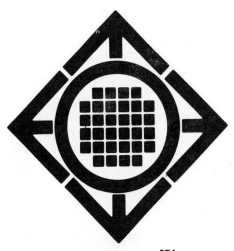

574

576

575

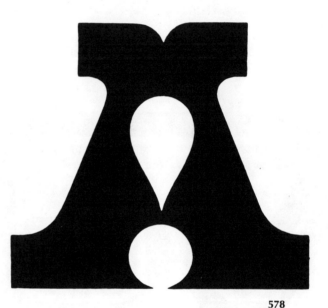

578

577

579

575. Mayflower Transit Co., Inc. Designed by J. R. Kaltenbach & Assoc. **576.** Ms. Katie Cohen, macrame artist and weaver. Used on her personal stationery and woven labels. Designed by Emil M. Cohen. **577.** Selame Design Associates. Designed by Joseph Selame. **578.** Action Associates, the advertising agency for Spectrum Sports Arena and the Flyers, Philadelphia ice-hockey team. Designed in 1970 by Mel Richman, Inc. **579.** *The New York Times*, a newspaper company with some 20 subsidiaries. Type-slug trademark designed in 1971 by Louis Silverstein, Corporate Art Director. **580.** Dover Litho, Inc., printers. Designed in 1971 by deMartin-Marona & Associates, Inc. **581.** Comlab, Inc., research laboratories, 1969–71. Designed by Dickens Design Group. **582.** Lathrop Associates, product development consultants. Designed in 1971 by Peter Muller-Munk Associates, Inc. **583.** McFarland Studio, Inc., photographers. Designed by Nancy W. McFarland. **584.** McFarland Studio, Inc., design. Designed by Nancy W. McFarland. **585.** Lowell McFarland, photography, 1968–70. Designed by Nancy W. McFarland of McFarland Studio, Inc.

580

581

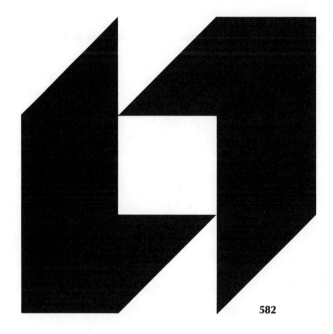

582

583

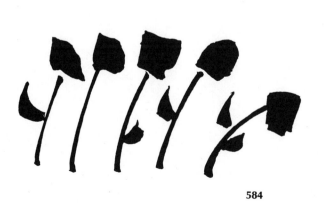

584

585

REAL ESTATE AND CONSTRUCTION

Perhaps because they are purveying intangibles, sometimes dreams that will never come true, real-estate marks are frequently strikingly original in their concept. Resort developments, particularly, use a very wide range of images in their trademarks. Being relatively free of franchise and tradition-laden considerations, their marks are often innovative in their manipulation of space and figure.

587

WILLOWBROOK

586

588

589

590

591

592

594

595

593

586. Rieder Haas Enterprises, Willowbrook Apartments. Designed by Mel Richman, Inc. **587.** Off Road America, construction of trail parks for use of motorcycles and other off-road vehicles. Designed in 1973 by deMartin-Marona & Associates, Inc. **588.** Conestee Falls, a development in North Carolina. Designed in 1971 by The Brothers Bogusky. **589.** Still Waters, land developers. Mark stresses wildlife preservation aspect. Designed in 1971 by Barrett & Gaby. **590.** Boise Cascade Corporation. **591.** Green Company, development and construction. Designed in 1972 by Barrett & Gaby. **592.** Amterre Development, Inc., name for Food Fair Properties, a shopping-center real-estate development company. Designed in 1972 by Sandgren & Murtha, Inc. **593.** King's Creek, condominium apartments. Designed in 1973 by Barrett & Gaby. **594.** Deck House, Inc., prefabricators. Designed in 1963 by Leverett Peters Associates. **595.** ·General Development Corporation, community developers. Designed in 1966 by Leo Burnett Co., using circle in square; revised in 1972–73, dropping square. **596.** W. J. Barney Corporation, building construction. Designed in 1972 by Robert A. Propper of Propper–Elman.

596

598

597

600

599

601

597. Joseph Haas Construction Co. Designed in 1972 by Mel Richman, Inc. 598. Homerica, a division of Homequity, Inc., realtors. At one time a knocker was given to each person who bought a home through the company. Mark developed by company originator. 599. Quillayute Camp, a private campground. Used primarily for signage; circle orange, wave shape blue, on dark-stained natural background. Designed by David Strong Design Group. 600. Coral Way Village, a condominium development. Designed in 1972 by The Brothers Bogusky. 601. Raintree Homes, Sunset Builders. Designed in 1968 by The Brothers Bogusky. 602. Portsmouth Parade, a redevelopment authority. Designed by Gregory Fossella Associates. 603. Universal Development Corp. Corporate mark for developer of new communities in Arizona. Design by Don Levy, President, Visual Design Center, an affiliate of Harshe-Rotman & Druck, Inc. 604. Melrose Homes, a condominium. Abstract M and rose. Designed by The Brothers Bogusky. 605. Acmat Corporation, interior and mechanical contractors. Original mark with figure, 1951; placed in house design, 1964; revised in 1968 by J. Burrill of the William Schaller Agency. 606. Chimney Hill Corporation, real-estate development. Designed by Robert A. Gale of Siegel & Gale, Inc. 607. Carl E. Erickson, builder. Corporate identity program. Designed 1970 by Dickens Design Group.

602

603

604

605

606

607

609

608

611

610

612

613

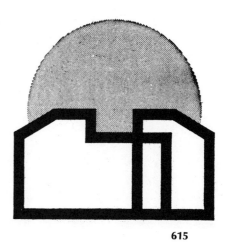

615

614

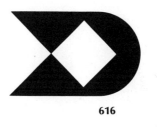

616

608. Kampgrounds of America, pioneer franchisers of camping space. **609.** Urbanational Developers, Inc., realtors specializing in component housing systems. Designed in 1972 by Jeffrey Swoger / Grafik. **610.** Lime Bay, a development of Leadership Housing, Inc. **611.** "Atlanta, New International City." Campaign device of the Economic Development Dept. of the Atlanta, Ga., Chamber of Commerce, 1972. **612.** Rainbow Bend, a condominium. Designed in 1972 by The Brothers Bogusky. **613.** Whittington, high-rise apartments. Designed in 1969 by The Brothers Bogusky. **614.** Ticor (Ti Corporation), title and mortgage insurance, property-development organization. Designed in 1971 by Saul Bass & Associates, Inc. **615.** Sunset Villas, luxury condominiums, a development of the Intercontinental Group. Design by Robert Myitray of Michael Sehack Advertising. **616.** Delsteel, Inc. Designed in 1970 by Mel Richman, Inc. **617.** Anderson-Stokes, Inc., builders and realtors. Sun symbol is black on yellow ground, waves are blue on white.

ANDERSON-STOKES, INC.

617

TRANSPORTATION

Transportation trademarks are important to consumers as well as suppliers because they function as foci of the romance of travel and adventure. Railroad, auto and airplane buffs avidly collect the old marks from the early companies, a hobby particularly rewarding in the case of railroads. The classic redesign of the New Haven, Hartford line (Fig. 648) in the forties started a trend away from shields and bull's-eyes, and toward modern typography; Illinois Central (Fig. 623) and Burlington Northern (Fig. 642) are more recent examples of this orientation. National Airlines' flaming sun profile (Fig. 627) is perhaps the most distinctive of the airline symbols, but all are constantly in use serving as directional signs in busy terminals, as baggage markers, on tickets, etc. Usage on the planes themselves seems almost promotional in contrast to the many other functions served by these marks. In the automobile field, however, the use of the trademark on the vehicle is much more important, but the retail function is vital too, as the trademark brings instant recognition to dealer showrooms.

618

619

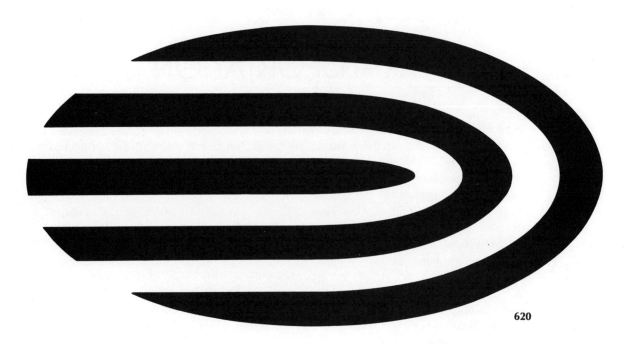

620

621

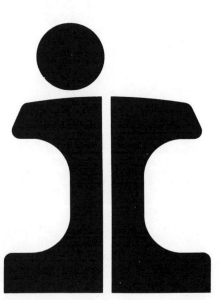

622

623

624

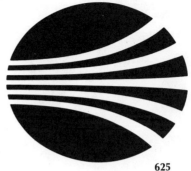

625

626

618. Greyhound Corporation, including leasing and financial operations. Still employs the dog used since 1914. **619.** United Air Lines. Designed by Raymond Loewy / William Snaith, Inc. **620.** Gate Lear Jet Corporation. Designed in 1967 (adapted from 1962 oval) by Carson / Roberts, Inc. **621.** American Motors Corporation. **622.** Pontiac Motors, General Motors. Used since 1907. **623.** Illinois Central Railroad. Usage: complete corporate identity program, company stationery and paper, rolling stock, vehicles, building and station signage, advertising and promotion. Designed in 1972 by Emil M. Cohen. **624.** TWA (Trans World Airlines, Inc.). Suggests the "biggest globecircler" of them all. Designed in 1950s by Raymond Loewy. **625.** Continental Airlines. Corporate symbol, part of an entire redesign program including unique timetables. Design also used on the "golden tail" of the plane. Designed by Saul Bass & Associates, Inc. **626.** National Railroad Passenger Corporation, an intercity train service. Arrow-shaped symbol is red and blue. Designed in 1971 by Wolfgang Rekow of Lippincott & Margulies, Inc. **627.** National Airlines. Usually seen in bright yellow and red. Designed by Tom Courtos of Papert, Koenig and Lois.

627

628

629

631

Cessna

630

632

628. Northwest Orient Airlines. 629. Convair Jet 880, Convair Aerospace, a division of General Dynamics. Designed in 1958 by Gould & Associates, Inc. 630. Cessna Aircraft. Mark evolved from dealer program in 1960; two red pennants, one blue. 631. Aerotech, manufacturers of aircraft parts. Designed in 1969 by The Brothers Bogusky. 632. States Line Steamship Company. Designed in 1956 by Walter Landor Associates. 633. Airborne Freight Corporation. Designed in 1965 by Walter Landor Associates. 634. Union Pacific. Shield, first used in 1887, was designed by assistant general passenger agent, Lomax. Today's shield is basically in the 1942 design, with the lettering in white on a blue background and red and white stripes. 635. Chrysler Corporation. Pentastar symbol. Designed in 1963 by Lippincott & Margulies, Inc. 636. Cadillac, a division of General Motors. Combination of the familiar shield with a "GM Mark of Excellence." 637 & 638. Pan Am. Old design (637), used from 1944 to 1957, reflected scope of routes. Design from 1958 to 1972, by Edward L. Barnes Associates, showed global scope of Pan Am. The current design (638) is by Joseph E. Montgomery III, Senior Director, Corporate Design.

633

634

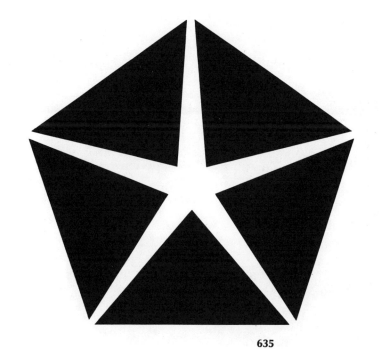

635

636

637

638

639

640

641

642

643

639. Eastern Airlines Corporation. Used with "Ionosphere" blue, a dark blue, and "Caribbean" blue (lighter). Change to new corporate identity program, 1965. Designed by Lippincott & Margulies, Inc. **640.** Grumman Aerospace Corporation and Grumman Boats. Both employ this trademark, suitable for both needs. **641.** Santa Fe Railroad. First trademark, 1888; present mark, conceived in 1897 by S. J. Byrne, passenger traffic manager, uses cross and circle of New Mexican Indian Christian faith. **642.** Burlington Northern Railroad. Interlocked initials set at slight angle to suggest motion. Designed in 1956 by Lippincott & Margulies, Inc. **643.** Uniroyal, Inc., tires. Revised design by Siegel & Gale, Inc. **644.** Goodyear Tire and Rubber Company. Winged-foot symbol used for all consumer and industrial operations. **645.** Nycal Company, Inc., custom rebuilder of bus and airline motor parts. Designed by Edward C. Kozlowski Design, Inc. **646.** American Light Aviation Company. Designed in 1973 by Sidney Dickens of Dickens Design Group. **647.** Southern Airways, Inc. Designed by Wolfgang Rekow of Lee & Young Communications, Inc. **648.** New Haven Hartford Railroad Company. Used in huge red, black and white letters on commuter and freight trains. Trend-setting design by Herbert Matter, 1948. **649.** Ford Motor Company. The well-known oval has changed in only minor ways.

644

645

646

647

648

649

UTILITIES, OIL, HEAVY INDUSTRY

Marks in this category involve great design challenges. The symbols serve many diverse functions, all combining in the end to invest giant, multifaceted, multinational corporations with personalities appealing to stockholders and retail and wholesale consumers as well as to employees and suppliers. Corporations such as RCA (Figs. 669–70), North American Rockwell (Fig. 730) and Westinghouse (Fig. 658) have tended to look for symbols that are ambiguous enough to satisfy members of all the several publics they serve. And yet some of the most memorable marks derive from more complicated earlier marks: Hercules (Figs. 726–27), Reynolds Aluminum (Fig. 659), A T & T (Fig. 654). Oil-company symbolism, like that for auto companies, is most tested by the standards of visibility, clarity and memorability in signage. Increasingly, corporate-identification manuals are being produced to standardize the many uses of these marks.

650

western union

651

653

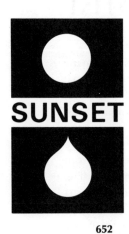

SUNSET

652

654

SUNOCO

655

656

657

658

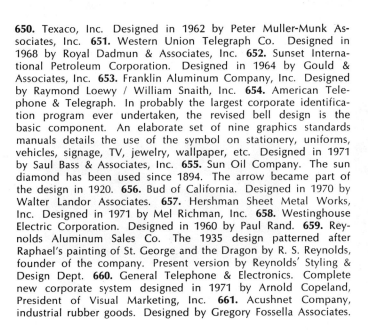

659

660

650. Texaco, Inc. Designed in 1962 by Peter Muller-Munk Associates, Inc. 651. Western Union Telegraph Co. Designed in 1968 by Royal Dadmun & Associates, Inc. 652. Sunset International Petroleum Corporation. Designed in 1964 by Gould & Associates, Inc. 653. Franklin Aluminum Company, Inc. Designed by Raymond Loewy / William Snaith, Inc. 654. American Telephone & Telegraph. In probably the largest corporate identification program ever undertaken, the revised bell design is the basic component. An elaborate set of nine graphics standards manuals details the use of the symbol on stationery, uniforms, vehicles, signage, TV, jewelry, wallpaper, etc. Designed in 1971 by Saul Bass & Associates, Inc. 655. Sun Oil Company. The sun diamond has been used since 1894. The arrow became part of the design in 1920. 656. Bud of California. Designed in 1970 by Walter Landor Associates. 657. Hershman Sheet Metal Works, Inc. Designed in 1971 by Mel Richman, Inc. 658. Westinghouse Electric Corporation. Designed in 1960 by Paul Rand. 659. Reynolds Aluminum Sales Co. The 1935 design patterned after Raphael's painting of St. George and the Dragon by R. S. Reynolds, founder of the company. Present version by Reynolds' Styling & Design Dept. 660. General Telephone & Electronics. Complete new corporate system designed in 1971 by Arnold Copeland, President of Visual Marketing, Inc. 661. Acushnet Company, industrial rubber goods. Designed by Gregory Fossella Associates.

661

662

SPERRY RAND CORPORATION

663

664

665

MARATHON ®

666

667

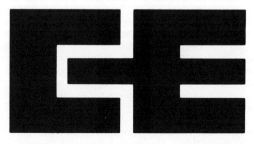

668

669

RCΛ

670

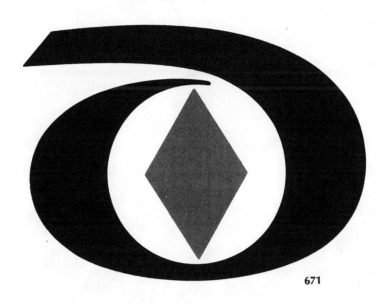

671

International

672

673

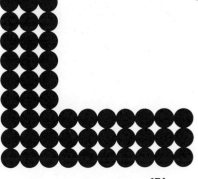

674

662. Mutual Oil Company, Inc. Figures tip their caps, suggesting service. Designed by Selame Design Associates. **663.** Sperry Rand Corporation. Designed in 1967 by Gerald Stahl, Inc.; revised in 1972 by 285 Design, a unit of Young & Rubicam. **664.** National Steel Corporation. N superimposed on coil of steel. Mark conceived by company in 1971. **665.** Badger Meters, water-measuring devices, valves and other products. The flowing lines of the B suggest water. Designed in 1971 by Design Consultants, Inc. **666.** Marathon Oil Company. Designed in 1962 by Lippincott & Margulies. The name Ohio Oil Company was changed and the Grecian marathon runner became the present modified hexagon with the M. **667 & 668.** Combustion Engineering, Inc., a manufacturer of energy-related heavy equipment. The old mark (667), CE and flames, was in use 40 years. New mark (668), with black C and red E, designed in 1970 by Donald Deskey Associates, Inc. **669 & 670.** RCA (Radio Corporation of America). Old symbol (669) and the new one (670) designed in 1968 by Lippincott & Margulies, Inc. **671.** Diamond Alkali Company, now Diamond Shamrock Corporation. Designed in 1958 by Royal Dadmun & Associates, Inc. **672.** IU International (formerly International Utilities). Designed in 1972 by Lefkowith, Inc. **673.** Crysteco, Inc., a manufacturer of metal crystals. Designed in 1969 by Peter Muller-Munk Associates, Inc. **674.** La Salle Steel Co., steel bars. Designed in 1967 by Morton Goldsholl of Goldsholl Associates, Inc.

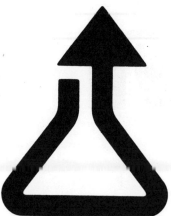

675

676

Purolator

677

678

679

680

681

682

683

684

EAT•N

685

675 & 676. Rohm and Haas, chemicals. Wavy line and monogram used from 1917 to 1965. Flask and arrow symbol and logo
by the late Lester Beall. 677. Purolator, Inc., manufacturer of
filters. Designed in 1973 by Schechter & Luth, Inc. 678. Perfec-
tion American, gear manufacturers. Designed by Morton Goldsholl of Goldsholl Associates. 679. Brunswick Corporation. Designed in 1972 by Morton Goldsholl of Goldsholl Associates. 680.
Superamerica Stations, gasoline and oil products. Corporate identity symbol. Designed in 1963 by Dickens Design Group. 681.
Dravo. Designed in 1962 by Peter Muller-Munk Associates, Inc.
682. Duquesne Light. Designed in 1972 by Francis R. Esteban. 683.
Pittsburgh Plate Glass. Designed in 1968 by Lippincott & Margulies, Inc. 684. Vaponics, Inc., water ionization and purification
equipment. Designed in 1968 by Gregory Fossella Associates. 685.
Eaton, security products and systems. Designed in 1971 by Lippincott & Margulies, Inc. 686. Malco Manufacturing Co., a division
of the Microdot Corporation, manufacturers of wire terminals
and connectors. Usage: complete corporate identity program;
company stationery and paper, packaging, building signage and
product stamping. Designed in 1973 by Emil M. Cohen.

686

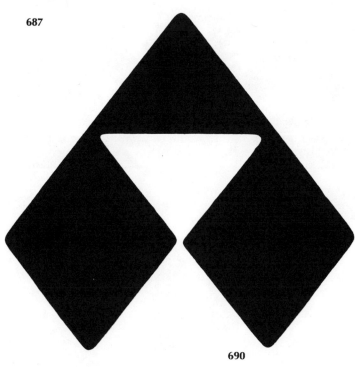

688

687

689

691

690

692

687 & 688. Brockton-Taunton Gas, a Massachusetts utility. Flame design 1971, by Selame Design Associates. **689.** Wynn's. Designed by Gianninoto Associates, Inc. **690.** Alcoa (Aluminum Company of America). Designed by Morton Goldsholl. **691.** Independent Telephone Company. Designed by Raymond Loewy / William Snaith, Inc. **692.** Carborundum Company. **693 & 694.** Mobil Oil Corporation. The corporation's dropping of its famous "flying red horse" was one of the most discussed design changes, accomplished over years with the help of at least three noted design firms. Pegasus, the Greek symbol of power, speed and imagination, was first used by a company affiliate in 1911. The present blue logo with a red O was introduced in 1966. Designers have been Peter Schladermundt of the Peter Schladermundt Co., Inc., who in 1956 convinced the company to start playing down Pegasus; Eliot Noyes; and Chermayeff & Geismar Associates. **695.** Southern California Gas Company. Designed in 1961 by Gould & Associates, Inc. **696.** Allen Woods & Associates, Inc., manufacturer's representatives specializing in the electronics industry. Usage: company stationery and paper, miscellaneous trade directories. Designed in 1973 by Emil M. Cohen. **697.** Sun Oil Company. The DX brand, formerly of Mid-Continental Oil, was acquired in 1955 with its diamond trademark. **698 & 699.** Shell Oil Company. A shell emblem was used since 1900, but the familiar scallop shell was first used in 1929. In 1961, Raymond Loewy / William Snaith, Inc. designed the new version (699).

693

694

695

696

697

698

699

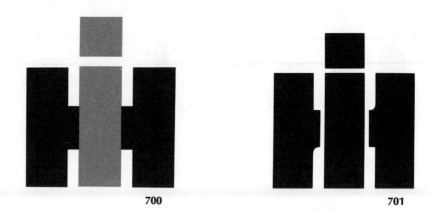

700   701

702

703

704

705

700 & 701. International Harvester, makers of heavy equipment. In 1973 deMartin-Marona & Associates, Inc., made slight changes in the well-known IH mark originally designed by Raymond Loewy over 25 years before. **702.** Johns-Manville, a multinational manufacturer of construction materials and supplier of raw materials. Began in 1858 as the roofing concern of H. W. John. In 1902, with the merger of the Manville Covering Co., the company name became H. W. Johns-Manville and a map trademark was used. In 1929, the JM monogram was first employed. In 1970 Sandgren & Murtha, Inc., "cleaned it up" for a "progressive" look. **703.** Fluidic Industries, manufacturers of valves and other industrial controls. Designed in 1970 by deMartin-Marona & Associates, Inc. **704.** Wisconsin Electric Power Company. Designed in 1969 by Dickens Design Group. **705.** Petroleum Consultants, Inc., oil-drilling investment counselors. Designed in 1962 by Donald Deskey Associates, Inc. **706 & 707.** Republic Steel Corporation. The new mark (706) is meant to be reproduced only in Republic blue or black. The lighter letter forms in the logotype ("steel") may be replaced by other product names. Designed in 1971 by Lippincott & Margulies, Inc. **708.** Houghton Chemical Corporation. Designed in 1967 by Selame Design Associates. **709.** Avisun. Designed by Mel Richman, Inc. **710.** Taylor Instrument, merged to form Sybron Corporation. **711 & 712.** Bethlehem Steel Corporation. Variations of this wide-flanged structural shape have been used since the 1920s. The dark ground was used until the 1960s, when the light ground was adopted, reflecting the demand for lighter, more modern steel products.

Republicsteel

706

707

709

708

710

711

712

714

PSE&G

713

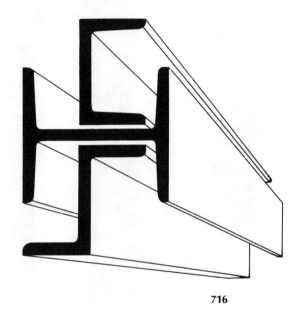

716

715

717

713. Public Service Electric & Gas Company, Newark, N.J. "Energy Burst" mark. Designed in 1971 by Gregory Ruffa Advertising. **714.** Kaiser Industries. Designed in 1960 by Frank Gianninoto. **715.** Missouri Auto Club. Designed by Raymond Loewy / William Snaith, Inc. **716.** Chicago Heights Steel, steel fabricating and supply firm. Designed in 1964 by Herbert Pinzke. **717.** Continental Steel Company, processors of solid steel into wire. Usage: complete corporate identity program; stationery, company paper, packaging, building signage, railroad cars, advertising and promotion. Designed in 1972 by Emil M. Cohen. **718.** Alcan (Aluminum Limited Sales, Inc.). Designed by Raymond Loewy. **719.** Allegheny Power System. Abstract A on a red ground. Designed by Sandgren & Murtha, Inc. **720.** Pennwalt Corporation, makers of chemicals, health products, specialized equipment. Designed in 1969 by Gerald Stahl, Inc. **721 & 722.** McGraw Edison Company, power transmission equipment manufacturers. The Thomas Edison profile trademark (722) was replaced in 1972 with a mark reflecting the new thrust of the company (721) designed by Melvin Miller of The Harpham Company, Chicago.

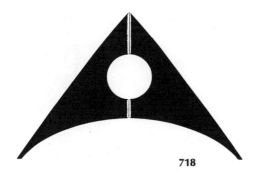

718

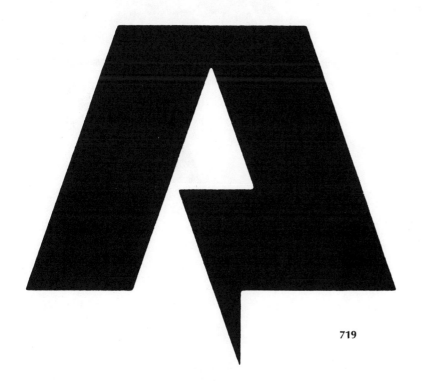

719

720

721

722

724

723

725

726

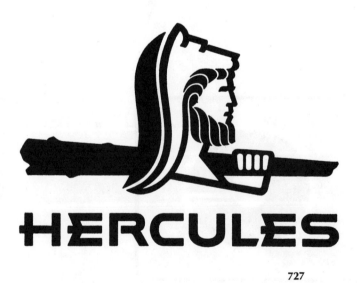

727

728

729

730

731

723. Exxon. In 1973, more than 25,000 gasoline stations put up new signs with the Exxon name. Design program by Raymond Loewy / William Snaith, Inc. **724.** Hallicrafters Company, electronic equipment. Designed in 1962 by Dickens Design Group. **725.** Peerless International, Inc., tool manufacturers and importers. Desgined by Jack Schecterson & Associates, Inc. **726 & 727.** Hercules, Inc. (name changed from Hercules Powder Co. in 1966). 727 was designed in 1963 by Gerald Stahl, Inc. The old figure of Hercules (726) was first used in 1877. **728.** American Gas Association. Designed in 1972 by Lefkowith, Inc. **729.** Public Service Indiana. When used in color, the lightning symbol is ochre. Designed in 1964 by Lippincott & Margulies, Inc. **730.** North American Rockwell, manufacturers of industrial components and flight controls. Mark symbolizes creativity, flight, rocketry. Designed in 1956 by Saul Bass & Associates, Inc. **731.** Atlas Chemical Industries, Inc. A globe is combined with the Greek letter alpha. Designed by Raymond Loewy / William Snaith, Inc. **732.** Motorola, Inc., electronics. Designed in 1955 by Morton Goldsholl of Goldsholl Associates.

732

INDEX OF DESIGNERS

References are to illustration rather than page numbers. It has not been feasible to include addresses, as many of the designs were executed several years ago and individuals and firms are constantly moving and/or reorganizing. Current addresses for most practicing designers can be obtained from the

Package Designers Council
619 Second Avenue
New York City 10016

and/or the

American Institute of Graphic Arts (AIGA)
1059 Third Avenue
New York City 10021

INDEX OF BUSINESSES, ORGANIZATIONS AND BRAND NAMES

References are illustration rather than page numbers. City locations are given only for a few very localized enterprises and products, and for concerns too small to be listed in trade directories.